WORDSWORTH

DAY BY DAY

Other Works by Jeffrey C. Robinson

Ed. Jeffrey Cane Robinson, *Keats: The Myth of the Hero* by Dorothy Van
Ghent (Princeton University Press, 1983)

Radical Literary Education: A Classroom Experiment with Wordsworth's Ode
(University of Wisconsin Press, 1987)

The Walk: Notes on a Romantic Image (University of Oklahoma Press, 1989)

The Current of Romantic Passion (University of Wisconsin Press, 1991)

Romantic Presences: Living Images from the Age of Wordsworth and Shelley
(Station Hill Press, 1995)

Spliced Romanticism [poetry] (Mellen Poetry Press, 1997)

Reception and Poetics in Keats: My Ended Poet (Macmillan / St. Martins, 1998)

Passione e Bellezza, translation of *The Current of Romantic Passion* (Liguori
Editore, 1999)

Co-edited with Roger Gilbert and Anne Wallace, *The Walker's Literary
Companion*, Breakaway Books, 2000)

Co-edited with Roger Gilbert and Anne Wallace, *The Quotable Walker*
(Breakaway Books, 2000)

The Life of Things [poetry] (TreeHouse Press, 2001)

A Wordsworth Notebook [poetry] (Mellen Poetry Press, 2002)

Amenia: A Memoir [poetry] (TreeHouse Press, 2002)

Unfettering Poetry: The Fancy in British Romanticism (forthcoming, Palgrave
Macmillan)

Co-edited with Jerome Rothenberg, *Poems for the Millennium, vol. 3: The
University of California Book of Romantic and Post-Romantic Poetry*
(forthcoming, University of California Press)

WORDSWORTH

DAY BY DAY

READING HIS WORK INTO POETRY NOW

Jeffrey C. Robinson

BARRYTOWN/STATION HILL

Published by Barrytown/Station Hill Press, Inc., Barrytown, NY, 12507, as a project of the Institute for Publishing Arts, Inc., in Barrytown, New York, a not-for-profit, tax-exempt organization [501(c)(3)], supported in part by grants from the New York State Council on the Arts.

Cover and book design by Susan Quasha

Library of Congress Cataloging-in-Publication Data

Robinson, Jeffrey Cane, 1943-
  Wordsworth, day by day : reading his work into poetry now / Jeffrey C. Robinson.
    p. cm.
  Includes bibliographical references.
  ISBN 1-58177-102-9
  1. Wordsworth, William, 1770-1850--Criticism and interpretation. 2. Wordsworth, William, 1770-1850--Appreciation--United States. 3. Wordsworth, William, 1770-1850--Influence. 4. Robinson, Jeffrey Cane, 1943---Diaries. 5. Poets, American--20th century--Diaries. I. Title.

PR5888.R56 2005
821'.7--dc22

2005018587

Printed in the United States of America

For Sam, Mimi, and Rachel

Preface

> ". . .winged words fly through much of
> Wordsworth's poetry, but,
>
> tradition, both from Wordsworth
> himself and in the massive march
>
> of his readers, has sought to keep them
> furled."
>
> (*The Life of Things*)

HOW CAN ONE HIGHLIGHT or recover the winged energies of Wordsworth's poems? Much of the twentieth-century's experimental poetics opens the eye and the mind to this possibility of a re-enchantment by removing Wordsworth from the formal and political prejudices that leave his poetry, for detractors and worshipers alike, "cased in the unfeeling armour of old time." In this book I attempt to locate resonances between the idioms of Wordsworth's Romanticism and the poetry of experimental modernism and post-modernism. To write that resonance seems like an intervention in which the poetries of each era interanimate each other along the lines of the principles of animation itself. And the goal?–like Ariel released from his arboreal imprisonment, to free Wordsworth's poems from the armored prison of the tradition of chasteness, of pastness–a poet of emotion recollected in tranquillity. He is rather the poet–at times in spite of himself–of "the life of things."

I will write in two mutually implicated genres. First there are
"Wordsworth" poems, new poems that I have written, often using his own
language and idiom but otherwise "original." Some of these have been
published before (from 1997 on) in collections of poems about and from
Romantic poetry and culture, and have been revised and re-assembled
for this Wordsworth book. Others I wrote amidst the diary itself. Then,
and primarily, there is a Wordsworth Daybook, which I kept for a year
beginning in August 2002. The book works largely by allowing unexpected
juxtapositions (of time, place, and poetry) to occur or by bringing analytic
observations to bear upon a Wordsworthian vitality, often missed in my
experience of the critical and scholarly literature. But the two genres–poem
and diary entry–strive to be one, really one poem, ranging expressions
of responsiveness that break through characteristically according to the
encounter of the moment. That "prose" from time to time transmutes to
"poetry" signals the willing relinquishment of ego-control over attempts
to understand the ancient materials. Dated entries root the prose speaker
in time, in critical controversies and traditions, in his own prejudices, in the
abhorrences (to recall the title of Ed Dorn's book) of our own day. Prose
commentary comes out of the highly labile mind of the quotidian. But
where does commentary-in-poetry come from? Who or what constellates
and authorizes the re-shapings of Wordsworthian language and images, the
juxtapositions ("splicings") of his words and those of other (often modern)
poets, the various minimalizations or spatializations of Wordsworthian
syntax, the stutterings and repetitions of his vocabulary? Authorization can
arise from the bed of world writing–e.g. George Oppen, the "Sayings of the
Fathers," Lyn Hejinian, William Blake, Ronald Johnson–weaving a cosmic
covering of knowing civility that now includes Wordsworth.

The mind of a reader, this reader at least, occupies multiple realities,
both in literature and in social, global, life. Typically these realities are
not compatible but are there nonetheless. Visionary poetry has long
acknowledged that simultaneity, beginning in the West perhaps with the
massive similes of the *Iliad* which, even though the Agamemnons on
the field before Troy try to keep the values of war primary, enforce the

proximity, in mind as well as in the cosmos, of war and peace: in the poem readers are not allowed to forget the fact and the values of one domain while the other appears momentarily more compelling. This rigorous habit of mind exercised by visionary poetry is one that I attempt to encourage in my reading of Wordsworth.

While "my" William Wordsworth (and I happily acknowledge a debt to Susan Howe's *My Emily Dickinson*, as well as to other pieces of "creative criticism") is primarily cast forward to the experimental poetries of the 20th century, it also reverts to the perceptions of Arnold and Pater that there are two Wordsworths: "a mere declaimer on moral and social topics; and he seems, sometimes, to force an unwilling pen, and write by rule," and a poet of "energetic and fertile quality...." Pater further says, "And this duality there–the fitfulness with which the higher qualities manifest themselves in it, gives the effect in his poetry of a power not altogether his own, or under his control, which comes and goes when it will, lifting or lowering a matter, poor in itself; so that that old fancy which made the poet's art an enthusiasm, a form of divine possession, seems almost literally true of him" (Walter Pater, "Wordsworth," 1874). In *Wordsworth Day by Day* I take this fitfulness and enthusiasm as axiomatic.

Although drawn to the spring-time energies of visionary poetry and poetics (as opposed to the elegiac poetics dominant in the schools, universities, and major publishing houses), I wonder how poets can sustain that vision while seriously acknowledging the traumatic "Real"–of the rape of Philomela and the dismembering of Orpheus–that cuts the flow of visionary waters of life from its sources. At the core of "my William Wordsworth" is trauma (early death of parents, the Paris September Massacres of 1792), overlaid, reinforced by *our* trauma (systematic attempts at genocide, serious nuclear threat, poverty, catastrophic global pollution, erosion of democratic principles), but I argue that his response in poetry is visionary (accommodating, transformative, animating, proliferative) rather than elegiac and consoling (substitutive); his poetry in its most energetic and fertile aspects is non-narrative and lyric rather than narrating predictable recoveries or completions. Such narratives we impose upon lyric

9

poems only to end up by "pre-reading" them (Jerome McGann) or passing them by.

How do poets respond to the dis-ease, the world brokenness, that they are handed? Wordsworth, perhaps more than most major poets of the 19th century, seemed pulled in both available directions: 1) that of re-making and re-envisioning possibilities, of defamiliarizing the tyrannical familiar and 2) that of erecting structures of consolations ("monument of unaging intellect"). But tradition has neglected or suppressed the former, and elevated or assumed the latter in the case of Wordsworth. This book teases out the former in a manner that proposes the necessity of the breaking of traditional forms, which invites apparently arbitrary influxes of unrelated materials an "opening" of the life of poetry. The unpredictability of the diary/poetry format repeats the condition of world-brokenness as a form, not of trauma and terror, but of play that seeks to enliven and free up the mind. Is Wordsworth the *object* or the *daemon* of these procedures?

These versions of juxtaposition and spontaneous reverie I hope will reveal what Wordsworth meant by the poet's only requirement, to "give pleasure" to his readers, the "grand elementary principle of pleasure."

WORDSWORTH

DAY BY DAY

August 2002–August 2003

August 10, 2002

IN "THE FEMALE VAGRANT" the early Wordsworth commits himself to the Spenserian Stanza to write about the poor. "The poor": what Louis Zukofsky gestures towards in his sestina, "Mantis." Wordsworth begins his career with an intuition about aristocratic form framing the poor, the artistic mystery of the cultivated mind deliberating upon the disenfranchised, a received coherence (Wordsworth's stanza, Zukofsky's sestina) in the presence of the disorganization of the referent, the entropy of poverty: a major fact or condition of modern poetry.

> The staff I yet remember which upbore
> The bending body of my active sire;...

Staff, line, stanza: a support but also a dialectic.

FOR THE LAST FEW DAYS I have been *worrying* a syllabus for my seminar on Wordsworth into shape—and feeling distant from both the class and the poetry. After spending a summer with Akhmatova and Mandelstam, with Horace's Odes and at another extreme Ed Sanders on America, the playful, witty, politically sharp Anselm Hollo, and with my own collage poems (Keats, Dante, Mandelstam), and then with the counter-poetics of Romanticism—Reynolds, Robinson, Hunt, Hazlitt—I look at Wordsworth who sits encased in lead. Vast slabs of poems, closed off, self-heated. And then the world. This summer seems out of control. The eerie global-warming drought in our city matches the horror of 1½ million Iraqis dead by "America's" hand. Corporate corruption feeds the world-wide water shortage. Threat of nuclear winter matches the roll-back in women's rights, and Bush closes his ears to life and love. The world grows numb when it doesn't feel hopeless. Wordsworth's power resides far from me; his politics and poetics double back on themselves in ambiguity. My syllabus, as of today, begins with early poetry and ends with late, with a month for *The Prelude* set aside. Yet nothing but frustration comes from this because I am leaving much out, racing through the rest. Then I read: "One of the functions of poetry is to bring people together, to pitch them toward one another with news about the poems which they both have read." (Allen Grossman, 1981) Something happened! du musst dein Leben ändern! How will we talk together about Wordsworth in this end-of-the-world aura? As I have walked this summer I think about the love of the mind playing with the beautiful Other that is poetic language—Levinas.

The line of poetry, that when looked at long enough lifts itself up like a serpent, looks around, and settles back imperfectly in its furrow! The words that cross over to death and incite you to follow. Poetry that has its source in rich soil and sparkling streams. "Wordsworth" for me is not the lyric subject, or rather it's not that poet-in-history, what "Wordsworth" has traditionally come to mean, from the beginning–the ego, the Lake District patriarch.

And I am back with Wordsworth, "my" Wordsworth of words, soil, and streams. It is significant that his door has been closed to me because I have been closed, presumably by our world and perhaps a bit hysterical with extreme poetries that, however, I also love, deeply admire, and want to emulate. But I've been trapped by Wordsworth the enemy when in fact he is the greatest teacher among the Romantic poets. The one who knows how to lose himself in the sources of life, in the *aquae caput sacrae*. Is this the beginning of a definition of Wordsworth as a writer? A definition I can help my students achieve?

Suppose in my class I begin with a section on Wordsworth and a poetry of the sources of life? *Then* move back to *Lyrical Ballads* and a social poetry? A narrative poetry. Then an autobiographical poetry or a *Tintern Abbey* and *The Prelude*, and a return to a poetry of stream and moon, that is, non-narrative lyric, at the end?

In this sense the value of his poetry lies in continuities, how treacherous the journey there can be, yet how comforting and enlivening. It's about the greatness of death, which aligns itself amidst the life of things—the animation in death and the world, the animation in the thing, which draws you to the thing, which then twists animatedly into new, deformed thought.

Closed form: Enclosure, as Clare said, is a kind of death. But in Wordsworth closed form is the threshold to the underworld of images. But we must not read him in sorrow or nostalgia or consolation, or as a progression whose utopia lies in an aesthetic future. The thoughts must twist and untwist (Zukofsky) until we become all thought and all observation and the image becomes a stream.

This diary streams, helping to see the unexpected flowings between poem and diarist, and within and from the poem itself.

I write like the child of Trilling, Hartman, de Man, but with the Russian modernists thrown in. History is the turbulence in a line of Wordsworth's poetry that is simultaneously rejected by God.

"BUT DEEM NOT THIS MAN USELESS." Wordsworth argues in "The Old
Cumberland Beggar" against the Poor Laws that seek to place the poor in
workhouses: better they should be allowed to live in a benign poverty, more
or less content and, by their mere being, giving pleasure to the community.
I wonder if Keats's irritation with Wordsworth's "palpable design" could
actually be an irritation with the idea of poetry as useful (as opposed to a
delicious diligent indolence). "The Old Cumberland Beggar" seems to me
a visionary poem until use floods the spirit of "wasteful expenditure." "I
saw an ancient Beggar in my walk." To see is not to judge or moralize: why
couldn't he have found poetry's ultimate social value in pure witness?

> And he was seated by the highway side
> On a low structure of rude masonry
> Built at the foot of a huge hill, that they
> Who lead their horses down the steep rough road
> May thence remount at ease.

Immediately in the poem the eye works in centrifugal contiguity. The
"eye's mind" (Karen Jacobs) makes the beggar, the sentence's subject,
superfluous to function, irrelevant to the rugged journey known and
anticipated, engaged by travelers midway in their lives. Yet the sentence
links them, binds them together in "one human heart." Sentence as heart-
image. The sentence announces the dissonance between the mind of the
poem, that connects, and images that refuse connection. The weakness of
the poem as a whole rests in its insistence to find a connection or continuity
where one likely does not exist. This feverish effort is goaded by the demon
of usefulness!

> The aged man
> Had placed his staff across the broad smooth stone
> That overlays the pile, and from a bag

All while with flour the dole of village dames,
He drew his scraps and fragments, one by one,
And scanned them with a fixed and serious look
Of idle computation.

Imagine that the poet maps idleness along a horizontal coordinate. Walking (moving rapidly down the page) belongs to others. The staff is laid down, momentously. It fills up an entire ten-syllable line…and then some. The same slowly filling of the line continues through a sentence that includes one long gesture beginning with setting walking aside, drawing food from a bag, and looking at it. This passage reminds me of Williams or Reznikoff or Niedecker: the old man turns waste (scraps) into something of value, something the eye ordinarily rejects now becoming a considered thing. The poem creates, insists upon, however, framing the moment in oxymoron: idle computation. (I originally misquoted the phrase as "idle contemplation," obviously not wishing to confront the juxtaposition of leisure and use.)

Such a precise and detailed sentence about observation! Such a mixture of surface and absorption, of motion and fixity.

(From the vantage-point of academic scholarship, a diary about a poet smacks of "waste" rather than "use.")

Old Cumberland Beggar (contin)

In the sun,

Upon the second step

Of that small pile,

Surrounded by those wild unpeopled hills,

He sate,

And eat his food

In solitude;

HE IS A STAR MAKING A CONSTELLATION, a set of cosmic correspondences in anapests and pyrrhics as well as iambs that take over while he eats. He resides in the sun, a Blakean human form divine, large in that sense but located, as well, with such precision: why do we see him on the second step? Occupying such a minute and exact niche? He "takes place" with such natural position, close to being a thing.

You could say he belongs to a cosmic "scattering" that begins in the sun and continues:

> And ever, scattered from his palsied hand,
>
> That still attempting to prevent the waste,
>
> Was baffled still, the crumbs in little showers
>
> Fell on the ground, and the small mountain birds,
>
> Not venturing yet to peck their destined meal,
>
> Approached within the length of half his staff.

The energy that comes from, belongs to him scatters strangely down his arm. The sentence, like the whole picture, is dispersive, blocked, gravitational: does he scatter or are crumbs scattered? The agent's agency is cloudy. The palsied hand has its own consciousness, an ecological one, at the same time a confused, baffled one. At the periphery of the beggar's world, the hand radiates its own equally uncertain consciousness: metonymy as winged representation, yet the displacement of consciousness may also signal its death in one sphere. Contiguity: domain after domain sit next to one another in a radiating influence and—in particular the hand and the crumbs—erupt the minor epiphanies into subjecthood, the life of these things! The operative conjunction "and" includes the small mountain birds, reactive. The beggar receives then gives, but the poetry doesn't quite allow for the simple moralizing economies promoted by serious theorists of the gift, of the argument for charity that encourages independence of indigents like this one. The scene is one of cosmic clarity and order but also cosmic confusions and (palsied) failures. Together you get combined a stunning materiality and spirituality, and a highly material poetics, or poetic shaping—of the strange balance of the staff that frames the whole passage.

I can't think of any poem that makes material observations so poetic—this palsied, failing figure emerges in such constructed elegance.

All of which comes together as an appearance. "Old Man Travelling," first version, is an appearance too, an appearance of a mind observing, selecting, fantasizing, judging. It begins:

> The little hedge-row birds,
> That peck along the road, regard him not.
> He travels on, and in his face, his step,
> His gait, is one expression; every limb,
> His look and bending figure, all bespeak
> A man who does not move with pain, but moves
> With thought–He is insensibly subdued
> To settled quiet: he is one by whom
> All effort seems forgotten, one to whom
> Long patience has such mild composure given,
> That patience now doth seem a thing, of which
> He hath no need. He is by nature led
> To peace so perfect, that the young behold
> With envy, what the old man hardly feels.

It looks like an "omniscient" observation, no apparent subjectivity or responsiveness. Then the poem abruptly switches focus:

> –I asked him whither he was bound, and what
> The object of his journey; he replied
> "Sir! I am going many miles to take
> "A last leave of my son, a mariner,
> "Who from a sea-fight has been brought to Falmouth,
> "And there is dying in an hospital."

Now the first part seems overly sentimental, even fantasizing a perfect reciprocity with nature and the world (like Rilke's Eurydice, "Sie war schon Wurzel"), "useful" to one who wants to aestheticize poverty. The exchange between them doesn't destroy the opening, but it does make it a partial portrait, and says something about the complexity of witness poetry, in particular, the biases and preconceptions of the witness that need overcoming: the clash and confusion of prospective fantasies and actual exchange. The only other Romantic witness poem like this one is Mary Robinson's "All Alone"—the tyranny or prospective fantasy as the only means of engagement, but with its need for corrections. The great witness poem needs to hold onto both! That Wordsworth later excised the exchange (the final six lines) is a failure of visionary poetics–also a failure to trust in the social and political necessity of testimony. Actually, I think that Wordsworth and other Romantics like Robinson, Barbauld, and Keats explore the poetry of witness and testimony as a crucial act of mind in the midst of social and perceptual shock: "Dull would he be of soul who could pass by / A sight so touching in its majesty," while "merely" about looking at London at 5 A.M., really criticizes the mind not yet attuned to the powers of witness. Poetry and witness: a perfect fit given poetry's affinity for acknowledging the Other.

September 4, 2002

THE WORDSWORTH OF *LYRICAL BALLADS* is much more Zukofskian than I, and most anyone I've read, have previously thought. That is, "Zukofskian" as his poems "Mantis" and "Mantis: An Interpretation" theorize the juxtaposition of aristocratic forms (e.g. sestina) with a content of social critique (e.g. "The poor") to create "thoughts' torsion," or "the twisting and untwisting of thought." The reader's mind twists between these two realities of vision. The poems about the old and the dispossessed struggle with versions of juxtaposition—with simple, elegant, venerable stanzas—in this sense. There is a wit, a critical consciousness put forward in the volume that gets passed over. The bedrock of balladic stanza form and the unruly, non-poetic subjects.

N.B.–Why don't critics and scholars, teachers of poetry, latch on to those brilliant and immensely useful Zukofsky poems that have so much to say about the form/content relationship from the perspective of a poetics of juxtaposition? More generally, why don't we read what poets say as "theory"?

September 6, 2002

READ "OLD MAN TRAVELING" in conjunction with "Lines written on a seat of a Yew-tree"—complementarity. If the lost youth were to write a "compassionate" poem, it may yet turn out like the first half of "Old Man Traveling," a poetry about a visionary imagination dominated by prideful self-absorption. This might result in the projective sentimentalism moving by "thought" and beyond poem, someone with almost no existence except in the Rousseauian sense of a *"sentiment d'existence,"* a trajectory of achievement that is a Eurydicean triumphant devolution to undifferentiation: *sie war schon Würzel.* In severing the witness position, does he define a poetics in which the self-enclosure leaps its own boundaries to a readership? Perhaps becoming a "mood of [his] own mind?" The reality of projective fantasy? But in *Lyrical Ballads* (1798) he figures the vision held of the old man as a failure of imagination because it fails in necessary knowledge. Such "innocence" is not useful, except as making available an affect for compassionate interest. Wordsworth is not as innocent as we think!

LAST NIGHT I HEARD ROBERT CREELEY read at Naropa. The large
audience was almost completely their faculty and students, to the point that
I—stamped intellectual University, by myself at least—seemed at first alien.
After two-thirds of the reading his voice became hypnotic, the line breaks
like curling waves, but unpredictable, but trustworthy, capping on a shore
of air. His prose—he read an early story—literally put me to sleep. But I
"arose refreshed"—for, among other things, *Helsinki Window,* a suite from
the early '80's dedicated to Anselm Hollo, sitting in front of him in the first
row.

"Helsinki Window" begins with an epigraph from Malcolm Lowry,
which has made me think of Wordsworth:

> Even if he were to throw out by now absolutely incomprehensible
> stuff about the burning building and look upon his work simply as an
> effort of a carpenter to realize a blueprint in his mind, every morning
> he wakes up and goes to look at his house, it is as if during the night
> invisible workmen had been monkeying with it, a stringer has been
> made away with in the night and mysteriously replaced by one of
> inferior quality, while the floor, so meticulously set by a spirit level the
> night before, now looks as if it had not even been adjudged by setting
> a dish of water on it, and cants like the deck of a steamer on a gale. It
> is for reasons analogous to this perhaps that short poems were invent-
> ed, like perfectly measured frames thrown up in an instant of inspira-
> tion and, left to suggest the rest, in part manage to outwit the process.
>
> **[from** *Windows,* **p.117]**

"Yet one more of these memorials." *Lyrical Ballads,* parts of *The Prelude,*
The Ruined Cottage and others take entropy, both natural and socially
determined, as the resistance against which poetry thrives—very Horatian.
That sacred bard countering the long night of oblivion, finding tears for

the *illacrimabiles* ("unweepable") hero before Agamemnon. It is interesting to imagine Wordsworth anxious that the entropy of the world belongs as well to poetry, and postulating to long poems with their multifaceted vulnerabilities, and that the quick inspired lyric frame (the fact of a poem's frame) reduces dramatically the odds for poetic decay; in Wordsworth's imagery, the little cells and oratories have a greater chance for survival intact, between night and morning, than the grand Gothic Cathedral in which they are housed. So that, for example, "the difference to me" in "She dwelt among the untrodden ways" refers clearly to the poet's act of praise ("fair as a star...") unweakened by the larger devolution that embraces both Lucy and the poem praising her. If the poem "suggests the rest," that is, the mysterious weakening of the blueprint, the poem itself doesn't embody it!—This is part of the complex mystery of Wordsworth's poems.

WORDSWORTHIAN tetrameter / trimeter:

Blank verse in *Lyrical Ballads* overflows the line in the image of "man speaking to men," secular, the social scale. But the tetrameter contains all. Congruity between line and syntax appears:

> It is the first mild day of March:
> Each minute sweeter than before,
> The red breast sings from the tall larch
> That stands beside our door.

> or

> A whirl-blast from behind the hill
> Rushed o'er the crowd with startling sound:
> Then all at once the air was still,
> And showers of hail-stones pattered round.

> or

> And all those leaves, that jump and spring,
> Were each a joyous, living thing.

Perfect containment and yet (in the last couplet) Reznikoffian transformation. Juxtaposition in rhyme, constellations through transcendent containment. . . or is it through the meeting of the forms and the phrases, a greeting from the abstraction of the great archaism of iambic tetrameter or trimeter to the emergent language? A small explosion of unexpected congruities. Congruence between syntax and line is supposed to bore. Maybe it's the animation (metaphoric) in the images, the verbs, that contrasts with congruence in a startling way. Is it absurd to think of these lovely Wordsworthian congruities and Levertov's "organic form" in which the line length is congruent with the breath?

I've tried in the past to startle the Wordsworthian line (and the line of much Romantic idiom) with a "splicing" of "Wordsworth" and modern or contemporary idiom. Hear, for example, Wordsworth and Celan, or Darwish, or Clifton sing their unanticipated authorities to one another:

> solitary raven
> which heaven's blue?
> Ravenswarmedover
> stronger whirring
> unseen
>
> > at this hour
>
> > > **(Wordsworth and Paul Celan)**

> This is the spot:
> the country of daggers
>
> > and nightingales
>
> > how mildly
>
> > > **(Wordsworth and Mahmud Darwish)**

What happens, in the above poems, to the playfulness of poetic speech and to the line when traumatic aggression, when genocide itself, surfaces among the birds and blue heavens? When the line–under these conditions– *breaks?*

universe is burning

its own darkness

sounding bows   Mandela

a dark wind is blowing

Azincour Poictiers Winnie

threatens the profane

a hundred years a dark

wind blowing with

unrejoicing berries

townships universe burning

inveterately convolved

serpentine on fire

death the skeleton blowing

burning A living thing

inveterate capacious

furnished in fantasy

locked....Huge trunks....free

(Wordsworth and Lucille Clifton)

Here the juxtaposition of Apartheid witnessed by an African American poet with Wordsworth's references to faintly felt "battles of long ago" in "Yew Trees" brings the latter into sharper focus, and disperses the former into the ghostly pervasiveness of gothic nature.

stone fall that morning from the sky
interposed between water and winding slope
johncrow sky   Girdle of rough stones
corner stone   Straggling   unhewn
heap   Fills my blood with deaf
leaf and spiderweb   unhewn heap
my mouth filled with beast and characters
no amen no soul no single stone lifted up
chiseled a name less neglect

(Wordsworth and Kamau Brathwaite)

Spinning still
I let incense grow cold
giving my body   Giving
idle since getting up
bedcovers tumbled
neglect   Neglect
spinning still
rapid line of motion
curtains down in the sun
upon my heels   stopped short
earth rolling with visible motion
tranquil as a summer sea
my body emaciated   a prisoner
neglected endless staring
sweeping through darkness
cliffs wheeling by me

(Wordsworth and Li Ch'ing Chao)

Male and female sexualities facing the melancholies in one case of discovering cosmic vastness and in the other of acknowledging the acute absence of the lover. The beauty of spinning pain! The precipitous beauty of the short line!

> Hearing thy short sharp cries
> Babbler with a tale of sunshine
> Begetting thy golden, wandering cries
> Modern, Babylonic cries
> Those lang'rous lengths of thighs
> O blessed Bird; we strain to listen, to touch.

(Wordsworth and Djuna Barnes)

We forget the sexually alive body in Wordsworth's absorption in bird-song.

UNQUESTIONABLY WORDSWORTH WROTE moments of visionary poetry, seeing the quickening power in things, anticipating Williams ("The Locust Tree in Flower") and Reznikoff ("These days...") and Niedecker (about April and the "yellows"). Re-read Ronald Johnson's *Book of the Green Man*.

The use of the simple verb as personification:

> In that sweet mood when *pleasant thoughts*
> *Bring sad thoughts* to the mind.

> To her fair works did nature *link*
> The human soul that *through me ran*;

> The periwinkle *trail'd* its wreathes;
> And 'tis my faith that every flower
> *Enjoys* the air it *breathes*.

> The budding twigs *spread out* their fan,
> *To catch* the breezy air;
> And I must think, do all I can,
> That *there was pleasure there*.

Last line practically Stein! Pleasure was: the poem ends not with an active personifying verb but with a copulative, which, however, gets its strength from the cloudburst of personifications. The speaker doesn't really act, but has a faith that allows him a witnessing capacity to go out of his own nature. The movement happens in language that is flattened into nature, into a *condition* (there was). Doubling the indefinite "there," pleasure rises to an essence, but—or and—in some sense, out of the activity of both twigs and minds, "pure imminence."

1) Deleuze—"The singularities and the events that constitute *a* life coexist with the accidents of *the* life that corresponds to it, but they are neither grouped nor divided in the same way. They connect with one another in a manner entirely different from how individuals connect."

2) Husserl: "'The being of the world is necessarily transcendent to consciousness…and remains necessarily transcendent to it. But this doesn't change the fact that all transcendence is constituted solely in the *life of consciousness,* as inseparably linked to that life…'"

The life of things = *A* life, singular, running through, spreading its inbetweenness. Is this the "Lyrical" in *Lyrical Ballads?* Does this life overflow or disregard the boundaries and terms of the aesthetic?

A life: these singularities prevent sentimentality in *Lyrical Ballads,* an interweaving of energies that pre-empt the connectedness made by sentiment controlled by the ego.

> These days the papers in the street
>
> leap into the air or burst across the lawns—
>
> not a scrap but has the gleam of life:
>
> these in a gust of wind
>
> play about,
>
> those for a moment lie still and sun themselves.

(Charles Reznikoff, *Jerusalem the Golden*, 1934)

IT'S REZNIKOFF'S USE OF THE SIMPLER VERB as the sign of personification and animation, the life of things, that marks the Wordsworthian lineage here.

> "...the green leaves seem to float in the air."
>
> "The trees have worn their leaves shabby."
>
> All day the street has been quiet" (as if at that moment it could burst into sound).
>
> "Not a branch sways" ("sways" is active, not simply the oppression of the wind's effect).
>
> "Only the leaves of the corner tree twinkle" (again, "twinkle" is animating).
>
> "leaf behind leaf the very night rings."

Float, have worn, has been quiet, sways, twinkle, rings: language is visionary, de-familiarizing: objects which we assume are at least acted upon become, through the quiet but irresistible and irrefutable verb, subjects, agents of movement and sound.

Reznikoff writes out of the Wordsworthian discovery:

> Love, an universal birth,
> From heart to heart is stealing.

The active verb, in Wordsworth, Reznikoff, Williams, Niedecker, marks the conversion, the waking up into "love," into "pleasure"—the condition and affect of visionary poetry. My recovery of these verbs from their mere, their nearly transparent instrumentality into their generative opacity gives me pleasure. I feel as though I have discovered a secret, but one analogous to that which Wordsworth proclaims: could my new observation steal from heart to heart, surreptitious yet in the open air?

From Reznikoff/Wordsworth, we come to Creeley:

> THE CART
> Oh well, it
> thinks.

Creeley: a minimalist Wordsworth, but as such he catches the noun as a scene of bare turbulence:

> WINDOW SEAT
> Cat's up
> on chair's edge.
> EYES
> All this
> color's yours.

> WEIGH
> Rippled refractive
> surface leaves
> light lights.

And this is Wordsworth's intuition: that the simple verb marks the turbulence within the simple noun. Cf. Niedecker:

> Popcorn-can
> screwed to a wall
> over a hole
>   so the cold
> can't mouse in

...never, never any where,

An infant's grave was half so fair. ("The Thorn")

FOCUS LESS ON THE STRANGE NARRATIVE and more on the juxtaposition: a mark of depth and tragedy worked in great fecund beauty, "lovely colours"! The bewilderment occasioned here grows out of the slow stubborn bewildering atmosphere emerging out of the superstitious community. But the poet in his "Note to 'The Thorn'," converts this juxtaposition into a principle of animating poetics.

In the note "superstition," ruling the atmosphere of the poem, which may be that which isolates permanently poor Martha Ray, and which creates a tempo of fear perhaps coupled with a collective sado-masochistic pleasure (i.e. good gossip) that is slowness approaching but not ever reaching the stillness of living death, stands in opposition to poetry, which in turn takes on the fancy-imagination opposition:

Superstitious men are almost always men of slow faculties and deep feelings; their minds are not loose but adhesive; they have a reasonable share of imagination, by which word I mean the faculty which produces impressive effects out of simple elements; but they are utterly destitute of fancy, the power by which pleasure and surprise are excited by sudden varieties of situation and by accumulated imagery.

Up from the earth these masses creep,
And this poor thorn they clasp it round
So close, you'd say that they were bent
With plain and manifest intent
To drag it to the ground;
And all had joined in one endeavor
To bury this poor thorn for ever.

Like the mosses on the thorn, superstition joins the gravitational forces of the mind submitting to the category of crime, isolation, and death, *adhering* to that category, mind with no independence, no agency and distance; the movement of such a mind is slow, leaning towards stillness. Wordsworth, with visionary intuition, proposes poetry as the counterforce to superstition, and the object of poetry (in "The Thorn" at least) to represent the slowness of the domain of the superstitious mind juxtaposed to the quickening possibilities of poetry and the mind-in-poetry (moving from "perception to perception"). The Fancy (mirabile dictu!) is the name for the quickening power and shows its effects through both content and form. His definition of the Fancy is very helpful (proving that Wordsworth understood the Fancy as well as any contemporary; indeed as not a typical poet of the Fancy, his definition and practice extends its possibilities in poetry): excitement, pleasure, mobility amidst variety and abundance of imagery. The poem, in other words, unlike the characters in the poem, extols mental and passional independence and liveliness, pleasure and play instead of a depressive fatalism. Wordsworth then states with an unclarity befitting the difficult nature of the subject, the intention behind this juxtaposition. He wants, first of all, to portray the superstitious type. But he intuits that the temptation to present them in their own terms would produce, paradoxically, a bad—that is, incommunicable—portrait:

> While I adhered to the style in which such persons describe, to take care that words, which in their minds are impregnated with passion, should likewise convey passion to Readers who are not accustomed to sympathize with men feeling in that manner or using such language.

They have, he compassionately avers, passion in their minds that, rather, are "impregnated" with it, a growing embryo of passion within the mind. How does one "convey" that passion to the Reader? First of all, note his concern for the reader, and note the use of the conduit metaphor: the passion in the superstitious is to pass across the barrier of the body and the barrier of the poem: just as Philoctetes cannot "convey" his pain, how does one "convey" one's passion? The poem must become the means to overcome the natural and social resistance, a point particularly brought home because of the emotionally self-enclosed members of the poem's atomized community. So, the Poet turns to a formal element of the poem itself, its metrics:

> It seemed to me that this might be done by calling on the
> assistance of lyrical and rapid metre. It was necessary that the
> poem, to be natural, should in reality move slowly, yet I hoped,
> that, by the aid of the metre, to those who should at all enter in
> to the spirit of the Poem, it would appear to move quickly.

Thus a transformation takes place, even though the same slow passion is conveyed, because in the conveyance of passion a quickening occurs, both in the necessary turbulence of the poem's form in relation to its content and in the experience springing up in the reader's mind upon "receiving" the poem: "rapid metre" encountering "slow faculties and deep feelings." "It would *appear* (italics mine) to move quickly": "deep feelings" encountering an appearance, that is, a *surface* and an *image*.

The voice becomes in the poem an *imago vocis* that, however, becomes the poem as an image of a mind in a state of quickening impregnating an *imago vocis*.

THOUGHTS' TORSION
THE TWISTING AND UNTWISTING OF THOUGHTS

a condition in which poetic form is indistinguishable from its content.

A condition in the poem towards stillness (the death of poetry) rejuvenates through the poem into never-ending, "sunny," mental motion.

NYC–MADISON AVE. BENCH AT 87TH ST.

WHERE DID WORDSWORTH'S MONUMENTALISM come from? Could he, in the spring or summer of 1802, writing about the butterfly or the daisy, have had any sense of the "palpable design," the institutionalization that a Mill and an Arnold and Pater would place upon these poems, turning them into an architectural construction? Monumentalism is a kind of virus, anti-poetic to the extreme, with which Wordsworth became infected, but when and how did it enter his system and poems? Imagine instead a condition of composition, in the Grasmere garden or orchard plot or on its hillside—the reclining poet summoning memories, playing with them, imagining DW's pleasure in his effectual homage to her for keeping him from tearing the wings from a butterfly. Perhaps it has been the air formed by the butterfly she saved that caused events—good and evil ones in balanced proportion—in our own time. The Twin Towers, says Baudrillard, were attacked symbolically (no one expected them to collapse) and then destroyed *themselves* physically. If we follow these events back in time, could we find the point where the representation of DW's gentle admonition that preserved life stimulated the sense of beauty, and love of motion and acknowledgment of life itself got torn to be replaced with the violence of the monumental?

Two hundred years (exactly!) separates me from that spring or summer day when monumentalism must have been far from the poet's mind, 200 years of reading and institutions, capitalism and more capitalism, war and more war. And now even more terror and suicide over the globe. The RAF blasts over and through the valleys of the southern Lake District! All images are symbolic, their meaning always already known, proposing erection and destruction of edifices. Does the butterfly poem belong to this extreme cataclysmic rhythm or does it stand apart? Can we return to a moment of the poem before the monument? Or, can't that pre-monumental poem pull towards us, pull us towards it out of the dark waters? Is its need for the monument's evil enough to violate the air of its own gladness?

At its most "perfect" (Adorno: "the more perfect the artwork, the more it forsakes intentions") the formalism in Wordsworth's lyrics creates their beautiful, stimulating surprises. But typically, his form induces in us complacent forgetting. So, let's open the form.

The poem of Spring and Summer 1802, in Grasmere, as butterfly, linnet; unchain the simile from its referent–give it a wing!

> Today's laughing
>
>   ease
>
> praise flowers
>   and birds
> reclining by waters
>   with similes

Give the butterfly a voice; let it ventriloquize Dorothy whom William had framed in rhyming tetrameters.

BUTTERFLY

1.

I settled
sleeping or feeding
self-pois'd on a
yellow flower

yellow pigment
distilled sunlight
thick   erotic
I heard hot waves:

"Stay near me–do not
take thy flight"
almost stopped unmoving
"float near me"–less
hungry waves

                        cooled me.

I know the voice
drank colors of death

2.

I thought
sadly with my wings
opening slowly
warming in sunlight
of the human scale
hovering still
saving
edges of the voice
My orange and black
scattered many
colors across
filling membranes.

3.

I am Emmeline.
I will grow as
Dorothy haunted

                        lonely with

wild passions which *they*
locate in my eyes but
which prick

surface of my lawny

                     skin at every point.

I will grow up

                     as gift of God

                     bereft,

so, cementing . . . facts,

I write

letters to other young women.

4.

Then Wm. fearing

catastrophe

of the familiar and

                     too proximate

celebrated *my* fear

of brushing dust

                     from interface of

air and butterfly wing–

We reassessed

   hunting and tearing:

ozone layer

I would not violate.

Insisting jointly (one day

lying breathing

                     together a full half hour) on

                     need for boundaries, we

re-named me

                     Emmeline

spreading these healthy chaste fears

on morning

                     sunny round of poems.

The tongue-entrancing
labial in my new name

                drew me to
waters of life from where
Wm's and my words
might kindle

        the entropied world.

Two years ago "Molly brought
   daisies etc.   which we   planted"
Now: arrangements of similes   derivations
   from first passions

                        naming
   plants   again   composing
             praise   dream profusion
             in similes   as wings

Daisy
           marked
opposes
           Great World
   joined with
     black and yellow
           flutters

                   weaves a
         Greater One

N.B.–I should write a poem that recovers in Wordsworth's daisy the atmosphere of harsh rural Scottish labor in Burns's "To a Mountain Daisy," the origin of Wordsworth and daisies.

> Lying on banks in tall grasses begetting begetting
> Again again the wandering cry lying together
> Still begetting breathing beloved wet songs
> Full fledged sparrows mouths closed so full
> Nests   dull evening   lying full close breathing
> Wm. met me lying breathing close the wandering
> Cry Cuckoo coo continually Wm. met me
> Wm. and I and swallows and thrushes employed lying
> Breathing breaking down failing lying down again
> Lying on sloping turf melting astonished
> On my couch like grave employed in bliss

Dorothy from the *Journals* lies with William whose mind is distracted by bird-song; but for these visionaries it's all–in spite of headaches and repression–one blissful task, their bodies entwined in an uncharacteristically (so we think) long line.

                              lying

> still   dances

>   flash   from

>   upon

lyingstillyingstillyingstillying
stillyingstillyingstillyingstill

lyingstillyingstillyingstillying
stillyingstillyingstillyingstill

lyingstillyingstillyingstillying
stillyingstillyingstillyingstill

A minimalization, à la Ronald Johnson, of the "Composed upon Westminster Bridge" sonnet in order to accentuate the ecstasy of early-morning sight–like Mirabai or the occasional ecstatic poem in the Greek Anthology:

Dull

So

        splendour

glideth

God!

The same game with a linnet in a tree:

sequestered

    guest

up

scattering

    glimmerings

flits

form

"...all good poetry is the spontaneous overflow of powerful feelings: but though this be true, Poems to which any value can be attached, were never produced on any variety of subjects but by a man, who being possessed of more than usual organic sensibility, had also thought long and deeply...such habits of mind...we shall describe objects, and utter sentiments, of such a nature and in such connection with each other...healthful state of association...."

THE CONDUIT METAPHOR, in this case, a poem carrying powerful feelings from deep inside the poem to outside spontaneously. So a poet doesn't precisely plan a poem, but it erupts and overflows—Homer-as-fountain. Yet poet is agent: we describe, we utter. Slippage: poem becomes poet, feelings become objects and sentiments, spontaneous overflow has a depth of habits of mind formed. Transformations seem to occur from that floor, that riverbed where habits and associations are laid down over time, inverted, a constellation of objects and sentiments overflow the precinct of the body and mind to become a poem as a constellation. How do objects and sentiments become feelings? The world and mind-as-world get laid down within. Somehow they erupt when one describes, utters. Perhaps a poem as product constellates inner and outer, chance and those layered habits, object, sentiment, feeling, power, describings, utterings, power, and feeling as an overflowing, as a Klein bottle of contiguities. Poem as a folding of all spaces, erasure of boundaries, cosmic unfettering even of word / referent distinctions. All as a giving pleasure. But where's the agency there?—

"there was pleasure there."

September 27, 2002

AN 1824 WORDSWORTH. Hazlitt thought the best, most original contribution from Wordsworth was the poetry of *Lyrical Ballads*. In his 1824 anthology *Select British Poets*, the Wordsworth selection of the "Living Poets" section has scattered throughout poems from *Lyrical Ballads* amidst the later poems. True, in the *Poems* of 1815 Wordsworth had inaugurated his categories of poetry by type of faculty, thus to a degree vanquishing chronology, but it's hard to read Hazlitt's ordering (what lies next to what?) without thinking that 1798/1800, the radical—poetically and politically— poet described compellingly in "My First Acquaintance with Poets" (1823) still lives for the Cockney sympathizer Hazlitt whose writing William Hone called a "political jewel house."

THE MORE I THINK ABOUT IT, the Cockney critiques of Wordsworth are at least in part misapprehensions, in the Bloomian sense of swerving from the true sources of poetic power in order to find space for their own poetics. So, yes to Hunt's invitation (*Feast of the Poets*) for Wordsworth to join his rural, absorptive poetics to an urban, impermeable one, and definitely yes to Hazlitt's wedding of the poetry of *Lyrical Ballads* (see previous entry) to the Cockney vision of poetry in *SBP*. Hazlitt, I think, knows, in "My First Acquaintance with Poets," the ambiguous image of Wordsworth, that a poet of the Fancy lurks beneath the encrusted poet of closed-form consolation from *Poems*, 1815. How difficult it must have been, given Wordsworth's haughty elitism, religious orthodoxy, and government income, to see the poet of "the life of things." How difficult to value the visionary playfulness, and play as part of the narrative mastery in *Peter Bell*, a poem so full of poetic freedoms in the very slowness of its verbal errancy:

> The Ass knew well what Peter said,
> But as before hung down his head
> Over the silent stream.

That kind of descriptive, visionary deliberateness ought to have been valued by the poets of the Fancy, but perhaps they were too much taken with poetic speed a la Olson. But they also misapprehended terribly the value of the simple, non-poetic subject.

COLUMBUS DAY. Now perceived as the day Europe brought death and disease, unwarranted, to this hemisphere. Two days ago the U.S. Congress gave the war mongers who are driving the world to destruction power to bring more death and disease to Iraq, to perhaps other parts of the Middle East, and—either directly or indirectly—to ourselves. I wake up—it's now the middle of the night—angry and terrified. And Wordsworth?—more "quintessential" as a poet than ever since one has difficulty knowing if he's on the side of liberty or oppression; does his poetry, does *any* poetry really urge wakefulness, as Charles Bernstein says—a *swoon* that wakes us up—or consolation and denial?

Wordsworth promotes the breath. Any "flower that breathes," or rather, let's get it not from memory,

> And 'tis my faith that every flower
> Enjoys the air it breathes.

And

> Spontaneous wisdom breathed by health,
> Truth breathed by cheerfulness.

One breath leads to another, indeed a "poetic" faith, as a breath in poetry leads to another breath. And I now will record, before the specter of pollution, or even incineration, how the image of the breath carries forward from Wordsworth into poets of the next generation that apparently vilified him—Hunt and Keats. But they showed their deep respect by reviving the breath as a mark of poetry's commitment to life, to being, to the sentiment of being as an elemental cheerfulness that runs through all things: if people, Americans in particular, let themselves open this baseline cheerfulness that poetry calls forth, the engine of death would have long ago been turned off. What does it mean that "breath" rhymes with "death"?

Hunt and Keats import "breathe" into their poetry from afar (from Wordsworth?); it belongs to an act of *re*-vision, of translation or carrying-across. Wordsworth's linkage of truth, breath, and cheerfulness comes to Hunt as a principle of Lake School poetics that the latter celebrates in the introduction to *Foliage* (1818). But the latter's epigraph to "Fancy's Party" in the same book, "breathe" appears as his translation of Manilius's *vivere*, to live:

> Juvat ire per ipsum
> Aera, et immenso spatientem vivere coelo.

> We take our pleasure through the very air,
> And breathing the great heav'n, expatiate there.

And in "Chapman's Homer" Keats revises, with Hunt and eventually Wordsworth in mind,

> Yet did I never judge what Men could mean
> to
> But never did I breathe its pure serene.

Here the two brash poets act not to oppose Wordsworth, as it often seems they are doing, but to fulfill, to carry across into the present, what they know is a major contribution in poetry and poetics. They take the next breath. And can we not then presume that a much more recent breath is taken by Olson, Creeley, Duncan, and Levertov in their poetics of projective verse? Will the word "breath" or "breathe" in the works of poets quietly marked since the 1798 "The Tables Turned" be the moment in each day since then that our current Satans cannot find?

October 12, 2002

[FROM NB ENTRY 12/30/01]

"THE CULT OF THE NEW makes an idol out of strangeness" (Nick Piombino). I idolize the strange as the elysium of de-familiarization. Time rushes by, and as I gather slowly the rhetoric to idolize strangeness, I see that strangeness has become the most familiar—as a concept. What am I left with? Is strangeness as tiresome as "subjectivity"? Do I like a poem because it startles me? Or does my response to its strangeness gratify because I know I'm confirming, entering my idolatry? Do I call something strange to mask a stimulating familiarity?

October 12, 2002

WORDSWORTH ALMOST NEVER greets me strange. The discovery or
acknowledgment of one of his beautiful personifying active verbs or the
nearly silent music of an enjambed line of blank verse feels more like the
sudden vigorous relief of a micro-*nostos*, a completing of the circuit in
which the errant swoon wakes me up:

> and restoration came
> Like an intruder knocking at the door
> Of unacknowledged weariness…
>
> Had glimmering views
> How life pervades the undecaying mind.

"the hour of feeling"—The most delicate of formulations, and most
strenuous for poetic thinking. "Thoughts that breathe, words that burn"
(Gray). An hour is a pretty good length of time, in spite of the almost
oxymoronic link of temporal limit and boundless affect, good expansive
spot of time. ABSORPTION. An extravagant amount of time: extra-vagant.
You can wander in and indulge an hour of feeling. At the same time, being
"the" hour, it may signal urgency and uniqueness, precious and not to be
(in dullness) passed by. Do all poems enjoin us to enter the present, to "sit
and eat" as the guest of the present? An hour-pool in which present and
past and future swim like goldfish. Look at the mild cheerfulness of the first
mild day. To forget its borders cheerfulness requires at least an hour.

Perhaps Wordsworth's moods, and his lyrical ballads, shocked, but now
they entwine the common-place with old forms, so that one can spend an
hour of mild feeling with them, sinking and lifting with the acuteness of
twisting and untwisting thoughts. "The cult of the new": *Lyrical Ballads*
must have been new, but maybe as Keats said, I should call them a "new old
sign."

> I should have mentioned that yesterday
> when we went with Wm to Mr. Luff's we
> met a soldier & his wife, he with a child in
> his arms, she carrying a bundle & his gun
> we gave them some halfpence it was such a pretty sight.

ON SATURDAY 18 NOVEMBER 1801 Dorothy Wordsworth observes, in her Grasmere Journals, that soldiers are "still going by," and this triggers memory of a vanishing scene from the previous day. A writer amazingly "unfettered" by conventions of syntax, capitalization, etc., as much as contemporaries Blake and Clare or the later Emily Dickinson, she must have silently agreed to herself (she must not have "quarreled with herself") to omit punctuation in the middle of:

> we gave them some half pence it was such a pretty sight.

She elides the economic consciousness, that led to giving money, into the aesthetics of scenic representation. She seems to mean that they—the soldier, wife, and child—were a pretty sight, but with no internal punctuation the "we" givers of charity belong, with no division or boundary, to the scene. Class differences are asked to vanish, embodiments of abundance and scarcity are asked to dwell in the same frame. By means of the absence of the semi-colon, she refuses to allow the neat separation of economics and aesthetics.

She writes (14 February 1802) similarly of a Highlander's daughter: "Her business seemed to be all pleasure." Transformation lies in the seeming, the appearance. The aesthetic not so much dissolves the economic but subordinates it.

> Her business seemed to be all pleasure—pleasure in her own
> motions—& the man looked at her as if he too was pleased &

spoke to her in the same tone in which he spoke to his horses.
There was a wildness in her own figure, not the wildness of a
Mountain lass but a *Road* Lass, a traveller from her Birth, who
had wanted neither food nor clothes.

Cf. Wm Wordsworth: "There was pleasure there." Pleasure penetrates
or blankets the scene allowing all figures, including DW, to melt into the
same animal wildness. Again, where is difference? Where is the Highlander
denigration or condition? Is it simply that poverty, that foreignness is
so taken for granted, so accepted that opportunity for a swim of and in
pleasures surfaces? "There was pleasure there" refers to nature which is
how the man responds (so DW says) to his daughter's light movements.

When she mixes business with pleasure, DW makes something where
only pleasure remains.

October 18, 2002

RECOLLECTION OF CLASSROOM CONSTELLATION of Poems: One Day
Yesterday an overload, and overdose of teaching poetry: three classes:
intro. to poetry, "Wordsworth," and Romantic Counter-Poetics Seminar
at U. of Denver (Keats); "metaphor" and "personification" in Shakespeare,
the Daffodils passage in DW's Journal and "I wandered lonely as a cloud,"
and *Isabella*. Tired as the day began, I stumbled through all three classes, no
whiff of poetry or teaching carrying over from one event to the next, the air
of fatigue too thin to buoy up figuration! In the middle of the night I woke
up, read an essay on post-modern elegy, and suddenly the vanished day
sodden with poems, "all at once," sprung into view not as a supersaturated
Dead Sea of image, drama, narrative, and line, but as discrete moments of
poetic success (and, less easy to register, pedagogic success). This morning
on my walk they arranged themselves as a constellation; teaching and
writing about Wordsworth in the Daybook, I keep returning to what might
be called his epiphanic personifications erupting primarily in verbs. Sheer
notation of the Life of Things. I now think that Hazlitt must have declared
with utmost sincerity his gratitude to Wordsworth for exclaiming in the
younger man's presence: "How beautifully the sun sets on yonder bank!"
and believing that the poet had taught him how to see into the Life of
Things.

Pass over the Shakespeare where we read a dialogue between Romeo
and Juliet at the end of their night together (was it the nightingale or the
lark that pierced the hollow of their ears?), a passage absolutely dense with
metaphor: I observed the conjunction of such density with being in love—
both metaphor and love translating consciousness to a different domain.

Shifting, changing domains—how and why they are marked and noted—
focus the distinction between Journal entry and poem. The entry works by
successive juxtaposition of elements and domains, the movement charged
by indices of response, query, speculation, and, as she says, fancy ("we
fancied…"). The world, as Bernstein would say, is opaque, as Trilling would

say, provides resistance, which is registered by contiguities. The broad highway of daffodils emerges somewhat gradually into what becomes an ecstasy of laughing and dancing flowers. Just as they walk through, she writes through the event, observing "straggles" of daffodils at the far end that, however, don't "disturb" its simple "unity." The passage, though moving through chronological time with apparent fidelity, is nonetheless composed and shaped.

Epiphany, if that is what it is, rises out of the opacity of a scene in the beautiful. In the poem it rises out of a vacant and perverse mood (wandered lonely as a cloud) and eventually takes its meaning and its renewal from that mood's recurrence—except indoors and far from the scene. The narrative belongs to spiritual time, "internal time consciousness" or a spot of time. If DW's method is contiguity, WW's is continuity, a point reinforced by the late addition of a new stanza two ("Continuous as the stars that shine.../They stretched in never-ending line..."). That line stretches from the initial wandering to his late bliss of solitude and his heart's dancing. In DW the moment yields unquestioningly to the next moment in history and in that sense vanishes unresistingly. In WW that final heart-dancing is nearest in time, of all the events of the poem, to the present and to the poem's reading, not only because it occurs at poem's close but because it is here where the best and densest metaphor-flashing occurs: "And then my heart with pleasure fills / And dances with the daffodils."

Does this final stanza define Wordsworthian closure at its most characteristic?—an insistent inwardness that contains all, but then flashes out, for an instant, within the bounded rhymes?

Ronald Johnson says that Wordsworth

> ...could not see
> daffodils
> only

'huge forms', *Presences* & earth 'working
like a sea'...

For William
there was only
one

wind off
the Lakes—

that, that had no
boundary, but entered

'skiey
influences'
into his pores

to animate some deep inner country
of deep, clear Lakes.

The Book of the Green Man, **pp. 15–16.**

So far I've been trying to write about this animation: the closed form is the deep, clear Lakes in which animation swims, happens, "Happily." But RJ is wrong to think that animation isn't part of observation!

"Is happiness the name for our (involuntary) complicity with chance?" (Lyn Hejinian, *Happily*)

Is Wordsworth's poem the memory of a chance? Is that elegy? And thus melancholy rather than happiness? Closure rather than aperture?

He doesn't say "Anything could happen" (Hejinian), or "I am among them thinking thought through the thinking thought to no conclusion" (Hejinian), but he says, "I have been there" and its value or "wealth" still enlivens me.

THINKING THOUGHT TO NO CONCLUSION: Wordsworth's hunger for animation rarely challenges or turns from physical and human realities: I think Johnson too easily shunts observation onto the genius of the poet's sister exclusively. In this sense Johnson's reading is absolutely traditional: I hope that my poems do not fall into this trap.

My final star in the constellation, Keats's *Isabella,* alters perspective radically, in the manner of a Cockney poetics: the background rises into the foreground, flattening perspective, narrative of romance—while held onto clearly—is at times subverted on the level of the sentence that can seem to take off, language in fact presents itself as fundamentally opaque and propulsive on its own—as if you took the Wordsworthian personifying, animating *verb*, that still serves its subject (the *flower* that breathes) and imbued language itself with that animation and independence.

The narrator claims he cannot tell Boccaccio's story with "the gentleness of old Romance,/the simple planning of a minstrel's song!" Gentle—at once without turbulence and twisting of thought and also aristocratic. The enemy to love in this poem is economic greed and the paranoid jealousies that accompany it. The evil brothers of Isabella oppress their workers (anticipating Marx's view, as Bernard Shaw observed) just as they oppress their sister by killing her lover. This economic consciousness flares up in the poem to the point that the narrator notes its intrusion on the simple transmission of Boccaccio to the present. Language thus becomes opaque as the poem expresses consciousness of living in a world ruled by the commodity. The narrator asks Boccaccio's pardon for language's refusal to lie down in an accommodation of transparency before the gentle tale of old.

> O eloquent and famed Boccaccio!
>> Of thee we now should ask forgiving boon...
> For venturing syllables that ill beseem
>> The quiet glooms of such a piteous theme.

"Venturing" can belong to the exploratory act of the speaker/poet or to the syllables themselves. In either case the syllables assume a texture and life of their own: animation has shifted from story and tradition to syllable, phoneme, sound. Moreover, they no longer fit with the melancholic gloom and pity associated with the original.

Watch the following syllables venture from the path of narrative as the brothers take Lorenzo to the forest to kill him:

> So the two brothers and their murder'd man
> Ride past fair Florence, to where Arno's stream
> Gurgles through straiten'd banks, and still doth fan
> Itself with dancing bulrush, and the bream
> Keeps head against the freshets.

Does the shift of attention from narrative to description parallel Isabella's mind that wanders from Lorenzo, even in death, to a pot of basil? The romance narrative itself seems to trail off into a haze of descriptors and madness, of permanent obsession with this replacement for love, which, however, has its comic side, a lightly ghoulish playfulness reminding the reader that one need not be captured by the narrative—imposed categories of gloom and pity. The poem, as Keats would say, ends in speculation or lively wonderment on the other side of murdered "wormy circumstance."

October 24, 2002

And very few to love.
Is shining in the sky.
The difference to me.

DEFORM "SHE DWELT AMONG THE UNTRODDEN WAYS" by making new
stanzas out of all the first lines, second lines, third lines, and last lines
respectively: This is the new last-line stanza. Doing this irritates people
who are consoled, in this case, by the lyrical-ballad quatrain. I understand
that. But I also like what I've just made, and how the word "difference" is
shorn of its questionably elegiac stature. Reading this I see the standard
assumption that the difference, to the speaker, of Lucy's vanishing has
little, or nothing, to do with lament, what I've always suspected, and much
to do with acknowledgment as praise and love in the presence of the near
absence of love. This triplet elides death and thus uncouples death from
difference, which now leaps back to a celestial shining but framed by love
intensifying through its growing scarcity. Intensity lies in a betweenness. A
further deformation of the deformation:

Love

shining in

The difference

TODAY IS THE 184TH ANNIVERSARY of Keats's chameleon poet formulation in which the poet, anti-Wordsworthian egotistical sublime, is said to have no identity and takes as much delight in an Iago as an Imogen. The speaker of a poem written by that poetic disposition becomes, as Deleuze would say, a "singularity" rather than an individual. This, as Oppen would say, is like a tiger in the woods without its scent, a creature unbounded by emotions and cathexes and by a local contingent biography. As Keats says, when I have been at a party not myself goes home to myself. And the poem (such a poem) similarly comes to occupy a place of "betweenness," unbounded, and in a sense form vanishes.

In a work of extreme pressure, Osip Mandelstam's *Fourth Prose* written as a knowing object of Soviet persecution, a line of a poem by Sergei Esenin is saved, i.e. acknowledged:

> There is a splendid line of Russian poetry which I never tire
> of repeating in the bitch-loud nights of Moscow. Which, like a
> spell, disperses evil spirits. Guess what line, friends. It writes on
> the snow like sleigh runners, clicks on the lock like a key, shoots
> into the room like frost:
> > ...didn't shoot the wretches in the dungeons...
> There is the symbol of faith, there is the genuine canon of the
> true writer, the mortal enemy of literature.

Wordsworth's value has always seemed partial. During Keats's time (e.g. Hazlitt, Shelley, Hunt) one distinguished his early "genuine" poetry from that corrupted by the Stamp Distributorship. Later Arnold distinguished between his relatively few peaks and his far too many valleys, and so on. Am I doing the same thing? For a poet often "cased in the unfeeling armour of old time," conservative form and the religion of the upper middle class, one must save the genuine poetry, the moments that Satan cannot find where singularity vanquishes individuality. You have to catch the moments—an anxiety felt and acted upon by Wordsworth himself—before they vanish. The visionary mantra would note that such a moment is, morally, every moment.

I realize that my Wordsworth is a poet of animation and personifications, that modern experimental forms (at least in poets like Creeley, Oppen, Niedecker. R. Johnson) animate form itself–that the line-break, the foregrounding of white space as unpredictable space, animates the line no longer complacent in its archaic bed.

But now here is the opposite: stretch the blank-verse line (of which Wordsworth is master) into a visionary fourteener, de-familiarize the archaic, make the line-animation struggle harder:

My Father's Death: Archaism (from *The Prelude*)

Single sheep and blasted tree an ordinary sight
follow his body to the grave anxiety of hope
too late the blasted hawthorne tree whistling single sheep
chastened and corrected before the three-horse holiday
desire by the old stone wall intensely gone to God
intensely straining sleety advancing body music grave
in wind and sleety rain in whistling anxious mist of hope
desire corrected follow body straining from the crag
choice feverish highest my half-sheltered father died
by deepest passion blasted bleak by chastened old stone wall
sorrow my brothers called expected steeds in mist to mind
of choice a long half mile a crag of passion traced
I should need long line repair return correct advance
in noise to God beat later workings on my unknown roof
elemental business of our single holiday
expect the steads anxious sight from fountains lately passed
long half line of working spirits spectacles and sounds
indisputable repaired the blasted sounds of God

October 31, 2002

"THERE IS AN EMINENCE" employs slow blank verse, personal, intimate, yet cosmic. You walk through it slowly, yet enjambment is buoyant and airy, points outwards, starwards, before the return to the next line:

> There is an Eminence,–of these our hills
> The last that parleys with the setting sun.
> We can behold it from our orchard-seat,
> And, when at evening we pursue our walk
> Along the public way, this Cliff, so high
> Above us, and so distant in its height,
> Is visible, and often seems to send
> Its own deep quiet to restore our hearts.
> The meteors make of it a favorite haunt:
> The star of Jove, so beautiful and large
> In the mid heavens, is never half so fair
> As when he shines above it. 'Tis in truth
> The loneliest place we have among the clouds.
> And She who dwells with me, whom I have lov'd
> With such communion, that no place on earth
> Can ever be a solitude to me,
> Hath said, this lonesome Peak shall bear my name.

A confluence of impulses, convictions, and poetic experiment intensified by the casual *immanence* belonging to the project of the "Poems on the Naming of Places," poems promoting topicality and the family, a domain in which domesticity has turned out from the home to relocate, through a name, on a periphery.

Blank verse: Rarely in Wordsworth does blank verse signal a celebration of casual walking and conversing, "saunter"ing, and yet this is the perfect image of Wordsworth's most peculiar use of this verse form—somewhere between a "public way," with glances drawn up—and outward, and a "rude and narrow causeway"; "Ill suits the road with one in haste." More than *Home at Grasmere* these poems celebrate the *nostos*—by enacting the lives of a few people in a beloved spot, or, the poems—particularly "There is an Eminence"—compose the new-old world as a constellation, a cluster of linking radiances.

Blank verse: stare at the poem as at a "graph" of someone walking—caesurae and enjambments for startings, pausings, and longer passages. Most lines lie down in peaceful, assured iambics: a rising meter among friends, around bends in the path. "Wordsworth takes a personal interest in the universe" (Hazlitt) in this blank verse, reaching from orchard-seat to meteors and the further star of Jove.

IN THE MANNER OF *THE ANCIENT MARINER* gloss seventeen years in the future, this poem offers a comedy of cosmic relations, animated and personified, only to declare the Eminence as lonely and then, by implication, to declare his own loneliness which he vigorously protects. The passion, or fervor, registered for Dorothy erupts almost like an Eminence, isolated yet constelled, tense and prayerfully intense.

There seems a confusion of clouds and earth and where *he* dwells. And in that blurring of domains there lies a vision of poetry as "betweenness," of something filling the spaces obliviating cloud for earth, earth for cloud— or the extremity of poetic dwelling for dwelling in the strong middle life. Blank verse, at least in their Naming Places poems, perhaps makes its own place stretching upward from quotation to cosmic, from passion-filled to a-passional.

"There is"—a locution of betweenness. How does one locate oneself between individuality and imminent "singularity," presence without subjectivity, without the poem and anxiety acknowledged in autobiographical representations? Blank verse: a verse form envisioning betweenness, in the congruence of language with the rising foot that paces past conflict, that interprets or imputes to the haunt of meteors a blitheness.

The Eminence is the "paradox of earliness and lateness" (Grossman), the condition of poetry as archaism. That which is "the last that parleys with the setting sun" is the first, newest, and most eminent for poetry, and in both cases outside the precinct of strong life. If the speaker identifies with the Eminence he would feel that loneliness of earliness/lateness and would have to construct a constellation including himself and love. The poem is that constellation, a spatial construct confident and blithe in its presentness as pure poetry if humanly anxious in its "depths" projected in words like "last" and "setting": the light is going out but not in the sure "rising" of blank verse.

There

        behold

           this

Is visible

        quiet to restore

The meteors

        so beautiful

             so fair

             in truth

          among the clouds.

She dwells

              on earth

FOR YEARS READERS HAVE CLUCKED disapprovingly at Wordsworth's slow erasure of the material poverty of "the leech gatherer" in successive versions of what became "Resolution and Independence"—from Dorothy's Journal entry to the manuscripts to *1807* and then finally to *1827*. The very present beggar observed by DW becomes eventually like "a man from some far region sent." But perhaps that blanket preference for the materiality of the leech gatherer's life, itself a swing away from "sublimity" in the older focus of readers, itself now needs questioning.

I've just noticed that the poem covers "three stages of life": 1) childhood 2) old age and 3) middle age. The speaker resides in the last, he appears metaphorically as the first, and the leech-gatherer himself, of course, claims the second. In these three stages enacted before us is the drama of a poet with the voices and the countenances of poetry, which makes "Resolution and Independence" about the poet's calling.

Begin with the child:

> I was a Traveller then upon the moor;
> I saw the Hare that rac'd about with joy;
> I heard the woods, and distant waters, roar;
> Or heard them not, as happy as a Boy;...

> I heard the Sky-lark singing in the sky;
> And I bethought me of the playful Hare:
> Even such a happy Child of earth am I;
> Even as these blissful Creatures do I fare;...

The "or"-grammar in the fourth line above is Wordsworth entering the child's inconsequence of choice; the next line ventriloquizes the child's easy delight in repetition (sky lark...sky")—the child: happy and blissful to the core. Wordsworth seems to have insisted on the "child" in him as crucial to the encounter with the leech-gatherer. Or rather, the child in him had come in conflict with the anxious, fearful, even despairing part of that within him embarking on poetic career. He has to identify with the *wunderkind* Chatterton poet, the marvelous boy who gives up life for authentic poetry. Or Coleridge, whose poetic authenticity is accompanied by helplessness in the world. Or Burns, whose authenticity lies in popular poetry, a line of which was a furrow ploughed "in glory and in joy" but that resulted in poverty and rejection. The child feeling at one with nature becomes the poet of truth but not the man of worldly engagement.

That man-poet travels through the world in conflict.

The strong man and the Old Man, Wordsworth comes to think, have to encounter each other in a purity, a necessary corroding of materiality, at the expense of the material truth of the actual leech-gatherer and of the poet who lives in time—beginning in *1820* Wordsworth omitted the following stanza:

> My course I stopped as soon as I espied
> The Old Man in that naked wilderness:
> Close by a Pond, upon the further side,
> He stood alone: a minute's space I guess
> I watch'd him, he continuing motionless:
> To the Pool's further margin then I drew;
> He being all the while before me full in view.

November 4, 2002 (contin. From Nov. 3)

THIS STANZA DESERVES OUR ACKNOWLEDGMENT! It is precise in its
Beckettian existentialist minimalism while it is precise in its spatial and
narrative detail. You could imagine it staged, at once embedded in and lifted
out of the quotidian, poised between vision and history!

When he omitted this stanza, Wordsworth absorbed and transformed
the Pool from a natural part of natural geography to one with a powerful
vertical axis: "Beside a Pool bare to the eye of Heaven." The leech-
gatherer now stretches out along this ascending coordinate, and heaven's
eye replaces the eye of keener human watchfulness and consciousness.
Wordsworth obsessed on the last line of the omitted stanza:

> 1) How came he here I thought or what can he be
>   doing?
>
> 2) He all the while before me full in view.
>
> 3) He all the while before me being full in view.
>
> and finally   4) He being all the while before me full in view.

"Full in view," unchanging in three versions, then vanishes altogether, as
if, by repetition, it comes to mean "unviewable" since, maybe, we only see
things partially in view, angled and perspectival.

> Close by a Pond, upon the further side,
> He stood alone: a minute's space I guess
> I watch'd him, he continuing motionless…

A minute's space, a spot of time, out of ordinary time, or rather poised
between history and vision, or a "betweenness," with shifting and unstable
referents—does the space refer to the Leech Gatherer.

November 5, 2002

[INTERLUDE IN "RESOLUTION AND INDEPENDENCE" DISCUSSION]

OF JONAS MEKAS'S BOOK OF IDYLLS, *There Is No Ithaca*, poems of an exile from Lithuania after WWII, writing idylls of his pre-war home:

> Now the slightest shift in the air brings on
> alder and juniper, over from the bushes,
> with young buds, new leaves, catkins,
> a smell of open water...

Do you need exilic distance to register that slightest shift in the air? Wordsworth knows such moments and cheerfully alludes to them, at home, because of being home: the flickering (unseen) of the green linnet in the trees near the orchard pathway.

OR TO THE GUESSING SPEAKER? Continuing motionless, "Dauer im Wechsel." Notice the floating "being," with "me" in one version and "he" in the other. If you imagine the poet halted "all at once" before this "being" but on opposite sides of the pond, walking *around* the pond to the Old Man, to keep him "full in view," you'd have to turn your head, a conversion in a minute's space.

The classic trouble in reading the poem with the knowledge of the "real" leech-gatherer, Dorothy's and his own in earlier versions, full in view. Yes, he leaves the social leech-gatherer behind, as he did *not* in the earlier "Old Man Travelling," But this is not a complacent fantasy poem, like the first paragraph of the former. Here he comes in touch with some "independent" movements of language and mind.:

> 1) the Old Man's words are independent of the man
>   himself:

>> His words came feebly, from a feeble chest,
>> But each in solemn order followed each....

>> The Old Man still stood talking by my side;
>> But now his voice to me was like a stream
>> Scarce heard; nor word from word could I divide....

And of himself: "My former thoughts returned...."

When in conversation with another, there is a sense of mutual control over what the other says, an unspoken agreement of civil obedience. But as the Old Man speaks in full response, in "courteous speech," "choice word and measured phrase," his interlocutor loses touch with their silent contract, his thoughts and listening regard dwell in a transformation from the materiality of speech and presence to language as stream, and the "whole body of the Man" "pac[ing] About the weary moors continually...."

A liveliness of vision overtakes the poet who gets in touch with what might be called the sources of life, the Old Man's speech and body converted from history to its pre-and post-historical revelations, a type and symbol of eternity.

I imagine Wordsworth in the minute's space of all these momentous revisions, perhaps not even fully aware of their significance for poetic calling, and perhaps in a poetic backlash lashing down the poem's closing stanza, but during the rich tumult of appearances and erasures, attempts to catch a poetic betweenness that he can't quite live with, finally. Such serious excitement, such serious play! And in a poem that features such a "rock-like, perdurable" figure, this poem sacrifices a bit of history for a lot of independence of moment and play of thought.

November 6, 2002

LAST NIGHT THE REPUBLICANS solidified their death-and repression-oriented anti-intellectual and anti-sexual stronghold over the American government and over all its people and me. More than ever, as person and as reader of poems, one must live in the present, remembering that there is a moment in each day that Satan cannot find. And at this moment I delight in the sheer fact of that just-discussed stanza that Wordsworth wrote and then cancelled and that I revived with my commentary.

OK, AN ENTRY I DON'T REALLY WISH to write: in the past few days
Wordsworth's poems seem texture-less, flat, airless. I think of bodies:
emaciated, atrophied, etc., etc. Was it a vision or a waking dream? An
illusion? Is there a there there? Puffed rice? Does his poetry inhabit a
domain, when you go there, do you convert to something? Do you engage,
as Felicia Hemans celebrated him doing, the deep sources of life?

Lately Wordsworth's seems an ideal poetry for deformation in the
manner of Ronald Johnson with *Paradise Lost*, which is to say that "the
infinite" (Blake) needs to be revealed "beneath" heavy-as-frost custom that
encases the poem. But with Wordsworth it's not simply formal elements,
diction, idiom that creates the problem, but could it be a relative reliance
on syntactical hierarchies, hypotaxis, the sense that meaning and value
do not inhere within the poem, so that it's not simply the "levelling" of
vocabulary, the reduction of poetic diction and tropes, but that difference
and juxtaposition, contiguity and metonymy, are not particularly central
to the poetics. This may trouble the value of a lot of canonical Romantic
poetry: when it becomes programmatically "absorptive" (Bernstein); only
"impermeability" allows for contiguity and juxtaposition; thus the great
success of a Keats who, though committed to absorption in new domains,
also insists upon texture in poetry (onomatopoeia, oxymoron) and on
parataxis. It's harder for me to see the *need* for deformation with a Keats, a
Mary Robinson, a Byron (hmmm, maybe Byron), than with Wordsworth.

I was led to write this now (although it's been on my mind for
almost a week) by re-reading Tom Clark's "Life of Keats," *Junkets on a
Sad Planet* which constellates Keats's quotidian life with the Orphic or
eternal one, managing to produce in the juxtaposition a version of that
Keatsian richness but, by emphasizing the contiguity (I think), not as
Keats would have done it. Clark collapses the prosaic and the poetic,
chronology into synchronicity. A value of this, even though it's in some
sense a familiar Keats, is that it challenges the Wordsworthianization and

Coleridgianization—that is, poetry as "self-realization"—of Keats. Could one do this for Wordsworth who desperately needs it? Or does he? Perhaps one needs to revel in the purity of Wordsworth's vision; one needs to travel away from his poetry from time to time, to recover its uniqueness. I keep *hearing*:

"there was pleasure there."

November 10, 2002

WALKING HOME FROM THE TRIDENT coffee shop where the last entry was written, I found that "there was pleasure there" kept "ringing in my ears." This led to "Nuns fret not at their convent's narrow rooms" and, somehow, from there to the perception that the interpretation of poetry in the British tradition is wracked with the elegiac on the one hand, and with "conflict" as a poetic virtue on the other, and that Wordsworth—in spite of a linkage to that reading practice—could be seen to propose an alternative poetics, far more modern than one would expect, based not on elegy and conflict but on "cheerfulness" and congruence. Or...he cheerfully envisions form as a capacious receptacle for content...or he brazenly, in your face, commits (and declares) the blasphemy that form is the container for the thing contained. He invites you into the house of poetry saying, "come, you will meet no resistance crossing the threshold. I am certain about the existence of the domain of poetry. Let me lead you there, and if you come willingly, you may have the experience of not knowing whether or not anything has happened to you. Think of it merely as a gentle pastime."

What he doesn't say is that he is elevating the "mood" to visibility for the first time in poetry, which creates a subdued confusion: if a mood is by definition of less importance for poetry than more public or religious generally sublime states of mind, then can you give it new visibility without a poetics of conflict, one that images the revolution of focus? But the formal revolution is, so to speak, negative: do *not* have formal conflict but quietly defy that expectation. You run the risk of "bad" poetry, but if it works, as it magnificently does in "Nuns fret not," then poetry has moved forward to a new sensation: poetry of mood or the scale of mood, involving the sleight of hand that says "In truth the prison, unto which we doom/Ourselves, no prison is." How far is it from this view of the sonnet to Denise Levertov on organic form (or Olson and Duncan) who want the line to fit the breath or the phrase—simply another way of cheerfully insisting upon form/syntax congruence. Cheerfulness indicates the affect of form and syntax greeting one another without conflict. For Wordsworth is also a vision of a labor that does not sacrifice human pleasure in the task:

> Maids at the wheel, the weaver at his loom,
> Sit blithe and happy....

Work becomes pastime, serious thought a sundry mood, and the sonnet helps to blur these distinctions, a fusion that recalls an Arcadian past but also anticipates an Elysian future (Schiller), and in this latter sense elevates the sundry mood to a conductor of a more integrated society. (Recently I was reading Hazlitt's *Table Talk* [1822] essay on Milton's sonnets where the sonnet also easily contains its content: no form/content conflict.)

I love to read this poem out loud to my students, to perform it with a quiet expansiveness of melody and rhythm. It's that expansiveness, moreover, that hints at its crucial association to the poetics of proliferation and contiguity—with parataxis dominating the first half of the sonnet and enjambment the second, along with an early *volta* (line 8 instead of 9) and rhyme variation in the sestet, all heard so quietly that conflict never enters one's consciousness. That such formal deception may be at work, or at play, imparts a low-key humor to the activity, a nearly untouchable acknowledgment that no poem, no matter how sundry the mood and pastime, isn't a construction. And perhaps it is this "Brownian" level that distinguishes this from a "bad" (congruence as boredom and banality) poem.

The poem manages the first person singular with equal tact, ushered in almost as an implicit invitation to an unaddressed reader to "sit and eat" at the table of the sonnet's pleasure:

> ...and hence for me,
> In sundry moods, 'twas pastime to be bound
> Within the Sonnet's scanty plot of ground;
> Pleased if some Souls...
> Should find brief solace there, as I have found.

November 11, 2002

WHAT DRIVES THE "IMMORTALITY ODE"? It opens in a classic instance of initiatory "dis-ease": "The things which I have seen I now can see no more."—twelve powerful monosyllables: definitive. But that in itself doesn't provide the prolonged drama of acknowledgments and inquiring that stays with the pain of near tragic recognitions. Instead, I propose, and in the growing spirit of my notes here, the moment of ethereal decision in the poem is also the moment stating at least the inner potential for a visionary poetry:

> Oh evil day! If I were sullen
> While the earth is adorning,
>> This sweet May-morning,
> And the Children are culling
>> On every side,
> In a thousand valleys far and wide,
> Fresh flowers; while the sun shines warm,
> And the Babe leaps up on his Mother's arm:—

Deform first paragraph of *The Prelude* (1805) à la Ronald Johnson, to "discover the infinite":

<pre>
                    blessing   this   breeze

gives.

                welcome

                    free,

                        sweet
murmurs
            Joyous,
            I look

                                        again;
                                            the mind
                Come fast
                By miraculous gift

                                        bold word
                            human
                                            delight
                                            turn

                            out
</pre>

Thus were my sympathies enlarged, and thus

Daily the common range of visible things

Grew dear to me: already I began

To love the sun; a boy I loved the sun,

Not as I since have loved him, as a pledge

And surety of our earthly life, a light

Which we behold and feel we are alive;

Not for his bounty to so many worlds—

But for this cause, that I had seen him lay

Its beauty on the morning hills, had seen

The western mountain touch his setting orb

In many a thoughtless hour, when from excess

Of happiness, my blood appeared to flow

For its own pleasure, and I breathed with joy.

Stammering: love the sun / loved the sun / since have loved him

Not as I since / Not for his bounty

MOMENTS OF INTENSE PRESSURE in Wordsworthian blank verse in which memory of past made conscious and full of significance "torques" the sentences of the present—*not* recollected in tranquility, not a smooth surface of a stream. This passage is at once patient in its meandering elaboration, exploratory—poetic lines like a snake moving through the grass, or something that "creates itself"—independent of the "I" that initiates its motion, but also has turbulent disorientations (which may be related to the sentence's self-creations) perhaps registered in the double personification of the sun laying His beauty on the morning and the western mountain—as if in a subsequent gesture of a *peopled* universe that includes the mobile sentence—touching the sun's setting orb. The stammering marks the disruption to the chronological narrative of sentences, a voice caught in a thickening vision of a boy immersed and stretched and imbued with utterances and agencies beyond himself. But since the stammering belongs to the poetic speaker, it reflects a view that at such moments of spiritual intensity the temporal separation is squeezed down to a condition of turbulent pressures in the lively vibrating, precarious sentence, which, it could be said, appears—like the speaker's blood—to "flow at its own pleasure." At its most shocking, Wordsworth's blank verse eschews the future-orientedness of that day when we will all be "free-standing agents," not "reclining poets" in touch with nature and reveries, but rather "aufrechter Gang" (in an upright posture of the citizen), in which our agency will flow like the most assured, and transparent, of enjambed pentameter lines; instead it stammers, calling attention to its materiality in the present, its ungainly reality.

The Life of Things (from *The Prelude*)

I was seventeen. I conversed conversed conversed with bliss ineffable coercive transferred sentiment of being and auxiliar light spread o'er spread o'er spread o'er beating living spreading gliding beneath wave and air life and knowledge and wave of air and melodious light with blessings spread around

half an hour I watched between mute with independent life (dust as we are) watched forms half an hour watched spreading archetype of numerous accidents watched ghastly forms breathless

I looked round ere I had been I left and saw I repaired and returned repaired ere I bowed low I should need . . .words. . .looked stumbling difficult dweller at bottom difficult and dreary stumbling invested vexed and tossed the girl blowing vexed and tossed

I cannot paint nor paint colors no colors and words unknown
sense of thinking beyond what I already know or what
   someone already
     knows is terrifying
words vexed and tossed unknown I cannot paint visionary
   dreariness in which   but the girl gone bones shaped like a
   grave

   that things of the lower
   world exist
   the world moves and remains

   naked pool

   emotion which discloses

   words vexed and
   scattered hair

   dreary the vision already
   "winter of the book"

   strong enchantment of
   dying away of stars
   I turn
               alone
     in gusty days

            fashioning
            fell destroyer

with gentle powers
slipping still hanging

from knotgrass
guided almost silent

strain of music
uttering
horizon

my mortal life on plain beneath gliding beneath the wave, now naked pool
that lay lonely scene beneath hills dim dim abode faint memorial gleam of
dim similitude having lain I register reascend bare slope trace

glittering idly
a cabinet of sensations

passion its birth
let the fiddler
scream in twink-
ling of stars

    *   *   *

    Daybook and poems: I have thought a long time about what seems the
tragicomedy of teaching a poem to students, teaching students—how to
say it?—"in the presence of a poem." The comic element is what Allen
Grossman calls the endless "sunny round" of conversation this teaching can
produce. The tragic: the difficulty of holding onto perceptions and lines of
thought made eloquent in the classroom. Poetic illuminations spreading
through the eloquence of minds animating my own observations. After class
it feels like dream or, more properly, reverie: you stand up from "le pente

de la reverie," you re-enter history from the world of images (descensus Averno), deep song. I write diary and poetry here in order to allude to shiftings of subject-positions evident in the "long school room" of talk in the presence of poems, where the "visionary gleam," "the glory and the dream" speak respectfully along side us children learning to cut and sew in the best modern way.

"Along side": the problem with Yeats's "Among School Children" is that teaching is going on at a pale distance from the site of profound meaning and excitement that erupts between the un-pedagogical inspector of schools and the collective images that the children evoke in him. The "room" of schoolroom talk in the presence of a poem fills with sunlight when what students say is allowed to become the "meaning" itself of the poem.

December 31, 2002

SIX WEEKS HAVE PASSED since I last wrote in this notebook; other projects and involvements and pure busyness have taken precedence. Wordsworth's poems, like rain, have sunk into the soil....

Almost half through Ken Johnston's *The Hidden Wordsworth*, I'm impressed with his account of the young poet's passions and his political complexities—I almost said "ambivalence" and/or "confusion," but those words make it all "his problem," so to speak, when in fact he belongs honestly, naturally, to both the conservative and radical sides. Beaupuy and he both arose from royalist and conservative religious parentage and held those sympathies instinctively: Wordsworth, for example, passing by Paris for the Royalist coloration of Orleans. And yet they are fighting together against poverty and aristocracy, for equality and liberty and community, and he fighting for culture and poetic language with its emphasis on difference and the image at the same time fighting for the "homogeneity" and "unity" implied and proposed in the pamphlet wars. Reading Johnston, though, I am learning to think less in terms of binaries and more in terms of a double helix of intertwining and intercalating elements. I think too that Wordsworth expressed his life that way in the early 1790s and perhaps at the end of the decade as well.

All this has meaning for a poem. Johnston sees *Lyrical Ballads* as a harmonizing of the warring elements. I see *LB* as still maintaining the double-helical reverberations. But a poem doesn't directly, or necessarily thematically express the psychological complexity. A poem shifts these matters to its own terms. What might be psychological agony can produce a shift in poetics, one that displays the double helix rather than chooses and excludes a part–cf. the textual history of "Old Man Travelling."

THE TRADITION OF READING WORDSWORTH since the principles of the Cornell Wordsworth (variorum) Series were laid down assumes that the poet's revisions showed a weakening of poetic interest and complexity from the initial decisions. But the revision of "She dwelt among the untrodden ways" turns attention from normative consciousness and biological history to a definition of visionary poetics. The first version, in a letter from Goslar from William and Dorothy to STC, opens:

> My hope was one, from cities far,
> Nursed on a lonesome heath;
> Her lips were red as roses are,
> Her hair a woodbine wreath.

"My hope" frames the poem with a metonymic link to the maid, defines her from the outset in terms of the speaker's desire, so that her death records the disruption of hope and desire, or its loss, which is how the final version is usually read. The first stanza also commits the speaker to blazonic cliches (lips like roses, hair like woodbine wreath) that drive him further into the space of personal desire. The phrase "from cities far" confirms a social identity, a rural one.

A fourth stanza, placed after the violet/star stanza at once insists on her biological history, her fatal pathology, *and* because of the primary authority of biology, the fundamental metaphoricity of the violet/star stanza:

> And she was graceful as the broom
> That flowers by Carron's side;
> But slow distemper checked her bloom,
> And on the heath she died.

The last stanza reinforces this one and presses home the common elegiac reading:

Long time before her head lay low
Dead to the world was she:
But now she's in her grave and oh!
The difference to me!- -

The revision of this poem is momentous: the struggle in politics, personal passions, and his sense of domestic responsibilities (with Annette and Caroline) gets played out in the first version on the field of consoling, normative vs. visionary poetics, the poem becoming a lyric manifesto of poetic vocation and value.

Compared to the first version, the published one seems like an abstraction, a "unity," as Barthes would say, meaning a dwelling in freedom, something unencumbered with grief, with personality, with history, with disease. Oblivion, or rather the acknowledgment of its immanence, occasions the poem and opens the way to the of praise, the "difference." Unlike the first version, the second waits until the last word to introduce self-reference. Up to that point the poem "dwells" in the world: a change in the world makes a difference to him, which he has already registered with an act of praise.

The poet changed "lived" to "dwelt," calling attention to the act of living-in-place: she moves from dwelling place to grave, the first as well as the last untrodden. The published version seems to elide life itself, becoming a "betweenness," the center of which, in the central stanza, directs us to see everything as a set of correspondences which (unlike the Lucy-less first version) is called "Lucy," a morning, rising star that radiates: intransitive.

FORM AS UNITY, TRANSCENDENCE, FREEDOM. Other poets may use the couplet more than Wordsworth, but his stanzas, often quatrains and five-line units, or more, are fully abstract, particularly when contrasted with his blank verse, so fully tied to the life, like a tree covered in moss. A dancing artifice of form: thus the brilliant corroding away of the personal in "Strange Fits of Passion" and "She dwelt among untrodden ways."

> A Violet by a mossy Stone
> Half-hidden from the Eye!
> –Fair as a star when only one
> Is shining in the sky!

Or:

> And now we reach'd the orchard-plot,
> And, as we climb'd the hill,
> Towards the roof of Lucy's cot
> The moon descended still.

The sense of dislocation in both poems partly arises from the lure, the formal grounding in perfect abstraction, slightly colored by the occasional trochee replacing an iamb ("Fair as," "Towards the") or by the nearly unnoticeable shift in subject ("we reach'd," "we climb'd" to "the moon descended still"). And the slight pun on "still," directing us to a continuation but also to stillness, an intensely non-narrative lyricism (in a very narrative poem)–a moon descending that does not move. Almost like the speaker sleeping "in one of those sweet dreams," the reader is continually nudged just across the border of the hypnosis of abstract form and rhythm and conventional images into a "border comedy" of liberated wakefulness.

HARRYETTE MULLEN SAYS about *Muse & Drudge*, "Despite random, arbitrary, even nonsensical elements, the poem is saturated with the intentionality of the writer."

John Cage says: "I am devoted to freeing my writing from my intentions."

Adorno (again): "the more perfect the artwork, the more it forsakes intentions."

Could one *ever* say this about Wordsworth? Absolutely. Congruences of line and syntax, moments when enjambment enacts the eloquent nature of reverie, moments when animation and personification are actually enlivened and made strange by form. When the lyric subject becomes mind-in-motion, unsettled in play:

> I try to put into verse my experience
> But my words only amaze me.

> **(Li Ch'ing-chao, trans. Rexroth and Ling Ching)**

> And I the day's coordinates.

> **(John Ashbery)**

Or, could I find moments, places, practices where and when he either lets "intention" go or where he points to such a condition?

The middle of "Nutting," parts of "Yew-trees," "Airey-Force Valley," "The unremitting Voice of Nightly Streams,"—how about various spots of time?—Are these moments when intention drops away, when for example those utterances are heard, or is that more gothic, more paranoid yet invoked and evoked from other worlds? In that mysterious late (1836) poem "Airey-Force Valley" the eye's mind seems led from observation to observation; or is it that words themselves lead, in conjunction with nature, but without reference to an "intending" human subject, from image to image?

> –Not a breath of air
> Ruffles the bosom of this leafy glen.
> From the brook's margin, wide around, the trees
> Are stedfast as the rocks; the brook itself,
> Old as the hills that feed it from afar,
> Doth rather deepen than disturb the calm
> Where all things else are still and motionless.

At this point "chance" enters, engaging the poetry-event and the nature-event, with its "even now":

> And yet, even now, a little breeze, perchance
> Escaped from boisterous winds that rage without,
> Has entered, by the sturdy oaks unfelt;
> But to its gentle touch how sensitive
> Is the light ash! That, pendent from the brow
> Of yon dim cave, in seeming silence makes
> A soft eye-music of slow-waving boughs,
> Powerful almost as vocal harmony
> To stay the wanderer's steps and soothe his thoughts.

I have the sense that there is a place where occurs the stochastic principle, in the sense that (Hugh Kenner) "A deterministic process…generated [the poem] with minimal interference, after crucial human decisions."

What is the relationship between intention in writing and the commitment to information, to "facts" (Oscar Wilde)? Scholarship and criticism in the Academy today seem committed to both intention and information, as if anything less would admit to a loss of control, internal and external. Certainly other issues count at least as much. The market, for one: what will sell, reward tenure, be-of-use. Sometimes I think that academic writing about literature and its world has itself become a principle of regulation rather than one of exploration, delight, uncertainty, intellectual risk-taking. Oscar Wilde in *The Decay of Lying* contrasting the great writers of the past with those of the present: "Facts are not merely finding a footing-place in history, but they are usurping the domain of Fancy, and have invaded the kingdom of Romance. Their chilling touch is over everything." Over the decades the retrograde version of Wilde's complaint became C. P. Snow's two-cultures debate, that trivializes Wilde's real point–the fanciful and romantic contribute vitally to the effective power of thought. Why shouldn't scholarship and criticism enter the orbit of literature's most vital elements? Swim in the same current? Haven't science, psychology, and "literary theory," to say nothing of generations of the world's great writers, shown up versions of disinterested objectivity as nothing more than a fantasy of control and regulations? Facts are obviously useful in the study of the life of a poem from the past, but not when their immobility becomes a final satisfaction.

The principle behind this book as well as much of my other writing is: the poems I like stimulate me to write–usually to write about them, but fundamentally, to write. Inevitably that also involves an engagement, an encounter with other writers about literature. But not slavishly or directly: the obliqueness of response, with its odor of anti-sociability, represents the lure of the image that, from Homer on, leads on into the shades, at best on a circuitous journey with the *nostos* usually a goal but not a certainty. Facts are epiphenomena on this human pathway, intention may initiate or stimulate but not regulate movement and chance, "all at once," encounters.

DOES WORDSWORTH THEMATIZE what Mac Low and Cage and Mullen convert into the life of language, syntax, structure? The "Life of Things" includes an independent quickening of form and language; Kinnell says Keats's lines, at least in the Ode to a Nightingale, rose like a Moslim at a prayer only to settle back down unconvincingly skew on their track or over it.

I'm imagining a three-part history:

1) As he pushes a horizon, Wordsworth hears, feels, sees the world come back at him from an "alien position" as a sound, an utterance, not precisely declaring intention but yet the mountain strides after him! At the same time "there are" utterances that, though irritated by the child's gesture at the boundaries, seem to be non-directive. So in Wordsworth otherness is and is not paranoid. Perhaps the "there is," "it is," "there are," which we think of in terms of being, are sites of randomness. The "crucial human decisions" generate poetry with "minimal interference."

2) Trees and torsos and obsidian stare at us as we pass by: Baudelaire, Mallarme, Rilke, Levertov. The sea turns its dark pages. All this poetry attends to domains other than those we control, but of course it raises the question of the sly control excited by positing the imagery of the beyond.

3) Language poetry and aleatory poetry talk about the "beyond" not as a domain but as a chance.

A FANTASY: IF YOU DEFORMED A POEM an infinite number of times, you would have the poem's ur-version. Or, the stream of poetry would total all of what we call its deformations:

1) Deform, as a chapbook, "She dwelt among the untrodden ways," to the point that it becomes scattered among the stars or hidden in the violet, moss, and stone.

2) Do an exhaustive study of the related rhizomes in *Lyrical Ballads*:
   a) "Description of a Beggar"
   b) "Old Man Travelling; Animal Tranquillity and Decay, A SKETCH
   c) "The Old Cumberland Beggar"

3) A possible comparative study of 2) and Mandelstam's "twins" (two separate poems, each revised out of an earlier, single poem) in his goldfinch poems

      Old Man Travelling
      Old Cumberland Beggar

      A Sketch-Animal Tranquillity and Decay"

Return:

   And very few to love.
   Is shining in the sky.
   The difference to me.

     love
      shining in
  the difference

  love. love; love:

  love: radiates
  love; couples
  love. constellates

   _____

     untrodden
  Beside
        None
   very few

Half-hidden
     a
   unknown few
    ceased

     love.
  Is shining
    to me.

She dwelt among the untrodden ways,
A violet by a mossy stone
She lived unknown, and few could know

       among

        mossy

           , and few

She
A violet

      could

She

             stone

                 could know

       among   ways,

         and

  dwelt
A violet
  lived   and   could

         untrodden
  violet   stone
She lived

Beside the springs of Dove.
Half-hidden from the eye
When Lucy ceased to be.

                         Dove

                 from

         Lucy

                 springs

                         the eye
                         to be.

                         the eye

                 ceased

                 the springs of

           Lucy

Beside   of
Half-hidden from
     Lucy

                         of Dove

                 from

                         to be

A Maid whom there were none to praise
Fair as a star, when only one
But she is in her grave, and Oh!
A Maid
           a star,

                                   and, Oh!

                         there

         is   only one

Maid   to praise

   a star

    in her grave

      there were

  star   only

But   Oh!

     none

But she   , and, Oh!

Fair   praise

   grave,

    whom   none

     only one

    in , and,

A. In the rhythm of:

    Lions, and tigers, and bears, oh my!
    Dwelt, Half-hidden in grave, and oh!

"The abrupt ending of the [penultimate] line with the gestural cry "oh" injects a sovereign implication that momentarily abolishes both meaning and subject; it is the one point in the poem where the material body inscribes a subject, not as a continuity or a self-consciousness, but as a pure operation of outlay. In the gestural cry, and in a manner similar to laughter, the speaking subject is utterly decommissioned, and language as a semantic, restrictive economy is put in question." (Steve McCaffery, "Writing as a General Economy," in *Artifice & Indeterminacy*, ed. Christopher Beach, Tuscaloosa: The University of Alabama Press, 1998, pp. 213-14)

B. "Abundant Recompense"

> Star ceased to praise
> Untrodden difference
> But mossy love dwelt
> Beside violet eye
> Oh! ways of love
> When stone springs
> When eye of stone is shining

> A commentary on deformations:
> I fly, my dust will be what I am."

Hafiz (quoted in Borges)

WHAT HAPPENED, COSMO-BIOGRAPHICALLY, to Wordsworth in writing "She dwelt among the untrodden ways"? Not writing; let's use his word, "composing." Placing it in stillness. Back again to the punctuation changes:

    1) And very few to love;   draft

       a violet, etc.

    2) And very few to love.   *1798*

       A violet, etc.

    3) And very few to love: all later editions
       A violet, etc.

Version 2 is the hidden Wordsworth, willing to let chips fall where they may, a juxtaposition, vulnerable to a poetry of associations as opposed to insisting upon control. Sexually charged, the first two stanzas lie side by side, as Dorothy Wordsworth would write of the two of them, breathing together. God resides in the interspersed vacancies of thought. Lucy is only a name yet to coalesce in voicing, power of sound, voice of light falling. Instead of recalling as a pale grief a pale memory of a pale person, he catches a falling star, a Lucy, not an evening but a morning and rising one.

Letting the versions lie and breathe side by side, we fall asleep with them and earnest questions of our existence arise like waves or leaves, as in Zukofsky's prayer to the moon:

> And, O moon,
> As we travail to sleep we do not know whether, with your
> genius furthering us,
> We should be counted as the cuspid waves of the seas, or
> as the souls of trees....

March 12, 2003

Where are we,
Mary, where are we?

SPOKEN NOT BY WILLIAM TO MARY WORDSWORTH but by George to Mary Oppen. "Art," said George,

> …may rescue us
> As only the true
>
> Might rescue us, gathered
> In the smallest corners
>
> Of man's triumph. *Parve puer*….'Begin,
>
> O small boy,
> To be born;…"

The earlier wife Mary (Wordsworth) "sent/to be a moment's ornament": A doubling, no, a raising to the 2nd power of those smallest corners, this in which a nothing of an instant being born.

"Blank verse…is an extremely dull medium to write in. Only the subtlest rhythmical faculty can ward off flatness for a long time. Perfect poems can be written in blank verse, that is to say, poems which can be read with interest and attention, and will fulfill and satisfy; but they must be short—"Tithonus," or "Ulysses" or "Oenone" and the like….Blank verse is the ideal medium for an unreadable epic poem."

Fernando Pessoa

PESSOA PRESUMABLY DOES NOT CONSIDER BLANK VERSE in terms of its origins, and some would say its triumph: Shakespearian drama. How to isolate and project a character at once engaging other characters on the plane of social exchange but at the same time reaching beyond the ordinary, familiar terms of exchange to draw together a larger view of the subject of the moment: blank verse, with its fixed meter and line length and yet with its potential for unconstrained thought (the enjambment). That tension exists in Wordsworth although the courtly community of exchange has been replaced by an implied pantisocratic one, and speech or thought turns intimate–from the domestic to the reverie; put slightly differently, relations between persons admit, as in a utopia, to no interpersonal barriers; poetic speech needs to leap no chasm of uncertain reception. Conventionally, critics have emphasized the blank verse association with epic, but the troubled relation to dramatic, "conversational" poetry must be recalled. But perhaps Pessoa is really talking about the fundamentally lyric character of poetry that blank verse seems to pass by, or through. At his best Wordsworth understands this problem, sensing the possibility of lyric arising out of the very "blankness" of the occasion.

During Autumn 1798 in Goslar, Germany, Wordsworth seems to have been experimenting—a kind of verse diary, a set of inner sketches, verbal watercolorings—with blank verse. A few of the experiments rose into

published poems–"Old Man Travelling," "Nutting," bits of *The Excursion*—
but most exist as a kind of water table rising to the surface of the Cornell
Wordsworth, a pooling of blank verse fragments.

> All beings have their properties which spread
>
> Beyond themselves, a power by which they make
>
> Some other being conscious of their life;
>
> Spirit that knows no insulated spot,
>
> No chasm, no solitude,—from link to link
>
> It circulates, the soul of all the worlds.

The first one-and-a-half lines exhibits the genius of Wordsworth's blank
verse, the spreading of spirit across the line-break, spirit that crosses the
chasm of resistance to connection between self and other which seems
the goal. The ten-syllable line indicates limit, the enjambment the hope of
connection but also of silent transformation, or trans-lation of spirit from
subject over to object (or other subject). One can see Pessoa's restlessness
with blank verse: the translation is quiet, not "disquiet" (Pessoa), and one
has to want to listen very attentively.

March 14, 2003

HE IS WORKING TO CREATE A VERSE FORM that already exists. Or maybe it is like moving into a new house, or as he would say, dwelling-place. "How do I make this place my own? How do I fashion myself in it? How do I insure that it will be a place of present activity but also possibility? I want to expand to the very walls and feel the cosmos. At times my blank verse seems the perfect vehicle for *writing* reverie, that has an onrush irrespective of the line: this is exciting. At times, blank verse for me being the formal image of the free-standing agent of democratic society that I want to depict: but that is a projection into the future, and when I'm thinking that way, the blank verse becomes declamatory."

Who lives here expands to the "human form divine" (Wordsworth as well as Blake); in those ten syllables the subject flows out to praise nature. In many of these lines blank verse resists closure, resists pastness:

> Come rest on this light bed of purple heath
> And let me see thee sink into a dream
> Of gentle thoughts till once again thine eye
> Be like the heart of love and happiness,
> Yet still as water when the winds are gone
> And no man can tell whither.

Rhizome

ACCORDING TO ALLEN GROSSMAN, blank verse at least from
Shakespeare to Wordsworth images the speech of the free-standing,
autonomous person. This seems precisely correct for the Wordsworth of
these experiments. "Experiment": how far can blank verse take me into
"philosophical" declamation and celebration? If that strange Portuguese
writer from the future visited me, he would have trouble maintaining
politeness:

> There is one only liberty; 'tis his
> Who by beneficence is circumscribed;...

The sentiment is right, and this condition is what I hope for poetry
and blank verse,...and I can't help myself. It's as if this language and ideas
run away with me in a kind of excess of moderation; I'm not listening or
observing, nor am I weighing words; I forget about animism, that "active
principle" of my verbs. But blank verse, with its line limit but its carefree
attitude towards end stop, beneficently circumscribes, and who wouldn't
want to build up that kind boundary, or dwelling-place? Besides, I feel proud
writing such lines. Saying this, knowingly, in verse:

> The love of order is a sentiment
> Inherent in the mind, yet does it seem
> That each access of strength this passion gains
> From human labours, by a course direct
> Or sinuous, is productive evermore
> Of littleness and pride.

An excellent statement, in an authoritative, economical way. A statement
about the "selfhood."

One important fragment in several drafts is the prelude to "Nutting."—
"Ah! What a crash was that!"—at once welcoming and admonishing
a young woman entering the grove. Female sexuality masked as
aggressiveness towards nature: perverse! "I would not strike a flower."
Again, not a convincing example of the anti-ecological impulse: it's not
about a destructive use of the natural world for aggrandizement. Even
"Nutting" itself, or nest-stealing, plays out such aggression on a harmless
scale: does nest-stealing really lead to concrete parking lots? And yet
admonishment towards, displacement of female sexuality and childhood
aggression, coming to us as blank verse, opens up moments, just moments,
of live visionary poetry of reverie, of actual revelation of the "life of things"
and of the mind. But rhizomes, "twins" as Mandelstam says. On this level
of momentary poetic openings Wordsworth composes by "ramification."
There appears no origin of a draft, at least of any significance, and no
endpoint in the spirit of the travelings. Poems, or passages of poems, seem
to open as pairs or triplets of versions, chunks of verse pass from one
passage to another, reappearing and self-remaking at the same time.

ON THIS GREY, DRIZZLING MORNING when the archfiend Bush and his fiendish collaborators prepare piously (pitilessly) for invasion, perhaps tomorrow (although the bombers are already dropping thousands of bombs), when their work is destroying not only lives but all the carefully and delicately if highly imperfectly constructed international agreements, to say nothing of world economies and trust, on this Thursday how am I to weigh the frail balancing act of Wordsworthian blank verse? How can beauty hold a flower against someone with all the money and particularly all the guns? Poets in the twentieth century pretty much consigned blank verse to a pre-Freudian, pre-Marxian, pre-Surrealist dustbin, but today turning to the "Discharged Soldier" manuscript, blank verse seems particularly antiquated—partly because it is about continuities whereas today the world at best is about contiguity: the poem sits next to the bomb and the Patriot Act. The individual, "Glad Day," limbs and senses, imagination capable of withdrawing its happiness or ranging freely in the zodiac of its own wit or exploring far other worlds and other seas (with what pleasure did I read these great lines in the Child Memorial Library at Harvard in 1963 and 1964, on a cool drizzly day far from home yet curled up in a soft leather chair reading by dim lamp-light, a time colored by the trauma of the assassination of President Kennedy, the bells tolling in Cambridge, the angry waves and cold, windy rain on Cape Cod beaches), the individual seems antiquated in its precise register of bird-like flickerings in a reverberant nature. Yet as I write those words the Discharged Soldier passage still convinces me that it speaks of reality—a reader in these terrible times carries the burden of prophecy loaded on Aeneas ascending from the world of loving images in the underworld—how, laboriously, to bring images to the troubled domain of the living:

> At such a time
> I slowly mounted up a steep ascent
> Where the road's wat'ry surface, to the ridge
> Of that sharp rising, glittered in the moon,
> And seemed before my eyes another stream
> Stealing with silent lapse to join the brook
> That murmured in the valley.

How beautifully the mind builds structures it can see! War, economic collapse, repression, the source in the 1790s of a soldier's decrepitude in some oblique manner weighing too on the speaker, seem far away. But the mind, traveling from observation of a stream to an apparition of one which he imagines connecting with a real stream further on, is developing its freedom through, in spite of or because of, that observation. Poetry in times of war serves the people by keeping the mind free.

> On I passed
>
> tranquil...

That "passed" occurs at the line break, itself a farewell to that line, signals a reversal of direction as well as a stepping forward, a resolution or fulfilling of passing in tranquillity. But what happens between the passing and the tranquillity? The line-break may assert that the tranquillity isn't purely a function of passing on, but is won, even constructed or, as Wordsworth can say, "composed"–no less real for that, indeed the insistence upon poesis when things are falling apart.

> On I passed
> Tranquil, receiving in my own despite
> Amusement, as I slowly passed along,
> From such near objects as from time to time,
> Perforce disturbed the slumber of the sense
> Quiescent and disposed to sympathy

With an exhausted mind, worn out by toil,
And all unworthy of the deeper joy
Which waits on distant prospect, cliff, or sea,
The dark blue vault, and universe of stars.

Beautifully the poetry's vision of the fulfillment of mind and soul in expansion both inward and outward stands at odds with the frozen affective and perceptual reality of enervation, as if the lines map two divergent pathways. The kind of oppression Wordsworth experienced in the 1790s when this was written dulls the senses and mind from its capacity for responsiveness, connection, assessment, and love. "Dull would he be of soul...." This numbness is an aim and result of repressive politics and a society intent on war (Nadezhda Mandelstam notes prevalent mental lassitude in Stalin's Soviet Union). Wordsworth's blank-verse poetry has its own aim of calling attention to a spiritual and mental wakefulness even when we feel encased in the armor of dullness. This passage, a prelude to the fully wakeful encounter with the discharged soldier, recounts pleasure received from "near objects" on the walk (poetic: a-MUSE-ment), a wakefulness in the slumber. Formally, the "disturb"-ance is just a ripple in the ten-line-long blank-verse sentence, which concludes with the (temporary) tragedy of missed connection to the "deeper joy" of a greater, cosmic wakefulness. Blank verse here is a lake; wakefulness the occasional fish leaping up to catch the insect and then disappearing; poetry catches the leap in the midst of the lake.

It occurs to me now that two major themes or concerns in this daybook —animation / personification and blank verse—are related contrapuntally: the enlivening, visionary element of lyric is often set in the (potential) oceanic boundlessness, or pre-consciousness, of blank verse. The two work together as a juxtaposition.

Some fine phrases on Wordsworth by Seamus Heaney in
The Essential Wordsworth **(New York: The Ecco Press, 1988):**

"almost geological sobriety" [cf. "Tintern Abbey," "Michael," *The Ruined*
Cottage, "spots of time" passages] The control over materials, that is,
comes from a slow source far outside the domain of the ego.

"Wordsworth's poems commemorate such an impression of wholeness and
depth"

"the note is sure, the desire to impress absent [precisely the opposite of
the centuries-long whine about the egotistical sublime], and the poems
thoroughly absorbed in their own unglamorous necessities" The sense of
poems, again, uninhibited by human anxieties and having an inexorable
drive. I see this in the way that his blank-verse sentences travel on their own.

[Of opening lines of the "Two-Part Prelude"] "Wordsworth's wide awake,
entering the thicket of himself like a readied hunter, as capable of deeply
receptive stillness as of silent, almost erotic foragings, forward and inward"
Consciousness is receptivity, availability to the other in spite of himself.
[Of characteristics of his blank verse] "its fluvial procedures, its murmur
that does not preclude declarativeness, its onwardness that does not
preclude sidewinding"

"that undersong of narcotic vowels and pliant consonants"

"his double bind between politics and transcendence, morality and
mysticism, suffering and song"

"He had grown up visited by swimming sensations of immensity, sensing communion with a reality that began where the dominion of his senses ended, and he was therefore inclined to accept the universe as a mansion of spirit rather than a congeries of matter." I don't buy the implication here of Wordsworth's anti-materialism: in the following three lines, it would be inaccurate to describe this strictly in terms of spirit:

[Wordsworth in 1790 France, quoted by Heaney:
    A homeless sound of joy was in the sky
    From hour to hour the antiquated Earth
    Beat like the heart of Man;...]

"masterpieces of disappointment" [Immortality Ode, Elegiac Stanzas]

"Cheerfulness," a robust, committed, and justifiably positive attitude in the face of evil and injustice, a comprehension that could acknowledge the ubiquity and affront of pain while yet permitting itself to be visited without anxiety by pleasure—this was the goal of Wordsworth's quest in the 1790's.

April 19, 2003

A homeless sound of joy was in the sky

TOTAL SUBMISSION TO THE IAMBIC METER, the sentence complete within
the line. What might be a banal congruence is here a perfect transparency
of form, or a releasing of the strange, buoyant content like an air balloon
over the France and England of Paine and Wollstonecraft, Price and Blake.

joy

home less   sound   sky;

in

constellation of hope.

joy

home less

sound

in   sky

April 20, 2003

ADDING TO HEANEY ON WORDSWORTH'S 1790 "chearfulness":
Lyrical Ballads, "the discharged soldier," deeply poetic in the sense that
"acknowledgment," "apprehension," far exceeds the witness's need
to be in control of knowledge and fate of the other. "We Are Seven,"
"The Idiot Boy," "The Thorn," "the discharged soldier" all explore the
willing intervention of the compassionate witness and the consequent
tensions for control over that fate of "neglected" otherness. The 1790s
witness-as-poet observes the "oblivious tendencies," not of nature but of
societal destructive negligence embodied in figures of wasting (soldier)
and suffering (Martha Ray) and are naturally drawn into the vortex of
constructing coherence which, of course, is what poetry proposes to do.
In these poems Wordsworth can acknowledge, describe, forgive (in the
Blakean sense of acknowledge and describe), and place within the aesthetics
of social contradiction (the economically secure speaker and the dissolving
other) while standing back from "resolution."

But what of the possibility of aesthetic coherence? I find, in the
"discharged soldier" passage, once again the Zukofskian principle of
"thoughts' torsion": "an uncouth shape," "meagre," "faded," "a desolation,"
"a strange half-absence," filling the lines of Wordsworth's blank verse.

April 21, 2003

WHAT COULD STAND IN GREATER CONTRAST to that half-absence,
dwindling from unstated trauma and social neglect, dis-charged as in utterly
without charge, that the sturdy confidence of blank verse, deriving from
Shakespeare and Milton and Thompson, the sign of the new democratic,
free-standing person? This contrast produces thoughts' torsion. Yet the
shock of the juxtaposition seems to be muted (as opposed to Zukofsky's
sestina about "the poor") because of Wordsworth's handling of blank verse
that seems to mirror the highly dynamic, very "thick" relations between
the two protagonists. Heaney's descriptions of his poetic line and words
helps me account for a certain anti-monumental cast in the formalism:
"its fluvial procedures, its murmur that does not preclude declarativeness,
its onwardness that does not preclude sidewinding." "that undersong of
narcotic vowels and pliant consonants." As Wordsworth deconstructs
Miltonic constructedness with the line's fluvial murmurs and side-windings,
he draws closer to the half-absence of the soldier, not, however, as absence
or weakness or indifference or immobility, but as the positive counterpart
of these things, an approximation of the soldier's enforced dwindling as
a presence of return to the sources of life which compels the speaker's
hesitant but ultimately interventionist sympathy.

April 22, 2003

THE SOLDIER COMES TO US IN THE LANGUAGE OF POETRY: measure,
foot, form, figure, murmuring sounds, voice, air, tale, word, sublime, tone,
theme, Discourse—thus reducing the distance between the domains of
life and poetry. How do we understand this witness as both actor in the
world and observer of it, one whose own speech functions on behalf of
the bereft, near-motionless soldier-without-charge but whose mind's eye
registers the man as object and image?

April 23, 2003

I'M HAVING DIFFICULTY WRITING ABOUT THIS PASSAGE; it's a density of concerns, a convergence: the soldier's vanishing, the witness's intervention, the witness translated into poet, poetry's substantiality, its secondary (inscripted) nature. So, I will quote:

> While thus I wander'd, step by step led on,
> It chanc'd a sudden turning of the road
> Presented to my view an uncouth shape
> So near, that, slipping back into the shade
> Of a thick hawthorn, I could mark him well,
> Myself unseen.

An encounter, yet at this framing point in the telling strikingly asymmetrical, weighted towards the subject, and yet not at all as ego, indeed is at best nascent, or flown, what "wander'd" must mean. Turbulence in simple verbs: "led"—at once past participle of "I" and simple past active of "step by step"; "turning" at once a point in space on a road and also the action of the road itself, so that the subject moves amidst other daemonically alive motions (personifications), a web or organism of movement directed ("purposiveness without purpose") towards encounter. Chance accumulates ("chanc'd," "sudden") into conversion ("turning"), the poetry recording the life-of-things that "present" the other to him, or rather "to [his] view." The initial "I," contained in a dependent clause, continues to depend, be dependent upon, other agencies and another (not directly at one with consciousness) registering instrument, "my view."

As the steps, road, and view assert their own agency, so the poetry "concretely," spatially, enacts the occasion, the surprise, with its own enjambing turnings: turning of the road... Presented, uncouth shape... So near. The blank verse reaches out to a poetry of aperture, where memory of the completed action dwindles before the participatory ("Present[-]ed") requirements of reading in this moment.

Presence in this encounter seems initially troubled by an economy of scarcity, something more than, or perhaps within, the practice of everyday life. Neither wanderer nor soldier is granted much definition, the former by slipping into shade (himself translated into apparition) and the latter having, paradoxically, a definition or outline unknown or unknowable. The archaism "uncouth" situates him at once in the distant past, coming from "some far region," and in literary language itself. The subject marks something unmarkable, in a sense more frightening, if less tragic, than what Blake's London wanderer marks. It is difficult to see anything at this moment of conversion, or switching to another order of reality. At the same time, reading with hindsight, it is difficult to locate the soldier in the world of every day life. The present participle "slipping" momentarily refuses to announce its referent—soldier or wanderer—proposing that each is inclined towards a vanishing at the moment of presence, a slipping into invisibility and non-presence. The tension or pressure at this instant is very high: the archaism may propose distance but the turning of the line suggests sudden and unavoidable proximity: "uncouth shape...So near." Similarly the phrase as limited by the line, "slipping back into a shade," describes translation from body and world into apparition, which, at the sudden line turning, snaps back into this world of nature, "the shade...Of a thick hawthorn." At the end of this claustrophobic turbulence resolution comes with the temporary invisibility of the wanderer relearning his ability to "mark him well,/Myself unseen."

"The Romantic Subject," if it exists at all, is constantly defined in its relations, in its capacity for absorption in the other, in its instability: the poet is a poet not in the home of the ego but walking "at the crossroads" (Tsvetaeva). In the following poem I quote Romantic subjects (from Keats, Wordsworth, Blake, and Clare respectively, and at the end Charlotte Smith), repeating them obsessively until the burden of the "subject" is lifted, like an illness, from my ideological shoulders.

The Romantic Subject

I wandered in a forest thoughtlessly I wandered lonely as a
cloud I wander through each chartered street I love to wander at
my idle will I wandered in a forest thoughtlessly I wandered
lonely as a cloud I wander through each chartered street I love
to wander at my idle will I wandered in a forest thoughtlessly I
wandered lonely as a cloud I wander through each chartered
street I love to wander at my idle will I wandered in a forest
thoughtlessly I wandered lonely as a cloud I wander through
each chartered street I love to wander at my idle will I wandered
in a forest thoughtlessly I wandered lonely as a cloud I wander
through each chartered street I love to wander at my idle will I
wandered in a forest thoughtlessly I wandered lonely as a cloud
I wander through each chartered street I love to wander at my
i d l e   w i l l
"tread" "and stroll" "and glide" "with faltering step"

SHAPE: MEASURE: MURMUR

From his lips, meanwhile
There issued murmuring sounds, as if of pain
Or of uneasy thought; yet still his form
Kept the same steadiness; and at last his feet
His shadow lay, and mov'd not.

...still from time to time
Sent forth a murmuring voice of dead complaint,
Groans scarcely audible.
Slowly from his resting-place
He rose, and with a lean and wasted arm
In measur'd gesture lifted to his head,
Return'd my salutation;...

...unmov'd.

...we must measure back
the way which we have come:...

Towards the Cottage without more delay
We shap'd our course;...

April 27, 2003

Perhaps it is the role of art to put us in complicity with things as
they happen."

Lyn Hejinian

"The writer over the page is driven down but like a robin by a
worm."

Lyn Hejinian

READING THE WORDSWORTH LINES I too am driven down into the
grave combination of the doomed repetitive mur-mur of groans and dire
constraint with that hand-mind of deft, compassionate measure shap'd
steadiness of poetry, which here is preceded by the protagonist rise out of
Hawthorn shade into questioning speech to the emaciated half-absence
of the soldier. Poetry dislodges the motionless, the stillness that bleak
colonialism has visited on the soldier. In the community at a short distance
from their hesitant encounter "fires all out" charge-less like the dis-charged
man, only the "yellow glitter" of moonshine in windows. Speech recovers
some of that charge, "a reviving interest," as I enter that complicity with
things as they happen.

Evening Voluntaries

1) "Calm is"-"Calm," here a noun, exists, or is defined by being.

2) "Calm is the fragrant air." Now become an adjective modifying "air"; or does "calm" modify "*fragrant* air"?

3) Calm is the fragrant air, and loth to lose

   Day's grateful warmth,

   The enjambment links "lose" to its translation into the next line, a conversion of a depletion into a new beginning, both in content and line position: "Day's grateful warmth."

4) "Day's grateful warmth, though moist with falling dews." This line, so increasingly rich, though shifting in its meteorological atmosphere and its vowel patterns ("a" to "o"), makes one forget the loss that guides this line, which simply builds like Keats's or Rilke's ripe apple. One of those chiastic nuggets of poetry (loss and gain).

From "Calm is the fragrant air" (in the manner of Ronald Johnson):

    favorite

          walk

Deserted.

A character

      Pathless   hour

            mounted

               watery I'd

              rising, glittered

                    eyes

                       to join

            exhausted

                    universe of stars.

            steal

My body

But sweeter far.   before

            round

Speak

Rose   imagery   now

           distant

                  dreams

          felt

          gentle

Eve. Vol. (cont'd)

> Calm is the fragrant air, and loth to lose
>
> Day's fragrant warmth, though moist with falling dews.

This last phrase opens something within fragrant warmth, at once an added element and a content *rising* out of an abyss, a betweenness, creating bounded space and distinction, all marked by

> The voice of the poem a wandering
>
> foreigner more strange
>
> and brilliant
>
> than the moon's   light the true
>
> native opening

(George Oppen, "Neighbors")

Pirke Avot

and Wordsworth

When he wrote about the *Pirke Avot* (Sayings of the Fathers) and its affinities to Wordsworth, Lionel Trilling concentrated on a belief in the celebration of mere existence, the power of silence, of mere being, as in Wordsworth's adaptation of Rousseau's *sentiment d'existence*, a formulation of a condition of life so elemental that it precedes, lies beneath human consciousness, social awareness, morality, and will. Critics have often criticized both Wordsworth and Trilling for a quietism, or contentment in cultivating or fantasizing a state far from social concern as manifested in visionary poetry. Yet both the Jewish Fathers (writing collectively over half a millennium ago beginning in 300 BCE) and the British poet writing in the immediate wake of the French Revolution show a second affinity, one which catapults into the present that reverence for mere being now given moral and poetical urgency. Two famous examples from the Rabbi Hillel:

1) If I am not for myself, who will be for me? And if I am
   only for myself, what am I? And if not now, when?

and

2) trust not thyself for the day of thy death; judge not thy
   fellow-man until thou art come into his place; and say
   not anything which cannot be understood at once, in
   the hope that it will be understood in the end; rather
   say, when I have some leisure I will study; perchance
   thou wilt have no leisure.

Hillel wants to guard against treating time as a rescue fantasy for avoiding the need to choose and act in the world now. Wordsworth's poetry, so often identified with recollections of childhood, shirks or transmutes the lure of the past for visionary apprehension, to the point that poesis of the present, so hard to achieve for anyone, seems nonetheless a moral and social discipline that the poet asks us to practice: to acknowledge "the life of things" right now, as it occurs and before it vanishes. He becomes a poet of the half-life.

And Trilling conjuring up this bizarre link between archaic Judaism and Christian/pantheist, psychologically modern Romanticism? The first Jewish professor of English at Columbia, in a trade then perfused with a blend of American nationalism and Christian humanism, finds a still point in his professional identity that speaks at once to his new audience of (largely) American academics, backwards to his childhood Hebrew lessons in the *Pirke Avot*, and outward, in a different coordinate, to the strangely gripping power of Wordsworthian art–what to call it?–the vitality "of mere being"? The genius to communicate epiphanies-in-solitude? Or perhaps Trilling is grateful for a poetry that represents the possibility of mind and soul sustaining themselves in a world of turbulent confusions and harsh displacements.

Naropa Reading—Introduction

MY READING TONIGHt is a selection from a project, now in the works for eight years, to reclaim the poetry of William Wordsworth for the visionary imagination. In the spirit of John D'Agata's notion of "essay," the project is at once an experiment in critical writing through my own poetry and diary-prose and a *weighing* of Wordsworth's work. No major poet has drawn to himself or herself the razor edge of parody more consistently than Wordsworth, the most recent in my experience being the BBC film *Pandemonium,* revisiting the history of the composition and publication of Coleridge's world of *Kubla Khan,* a history in which Wordsworth appears as the George Bush, the covering cherub or dark selfhood of the poetic imagination, and whose own poetic talent is rendered absurd by Byron inviting Wordsworth mockingly in a Regency drawing room scene: "come, William, give us a bit of your "Daffodils": how does it begin?—I wandered lonely as a... *cow?*" But you can find plenty to counter the common image of this poet, to paraphrase Wordsworth himself, cased in the unfeeling armor of old forms and religious orthodoxy. The poet that absolutely captivated his more radical contemporaries in poetry, like Keats and Shelley and even Byron, is registered by the great culture critic of the Romantic Period William Hazlitt, who recalls his first acquaintance with him in 1798:

> There was something of a roll, a lounge in his gait, not
> unlike his own Peter Bell. There was a severe, worn pressure
> of thought about his temples, a fire in his eye (as if he saw
> something in objects more than the outward appearance), an
> intense high narrow forehead, a Roman nose, cheeks furrowed
> by strong purpose and feeling, and a convulsive inclination to
> laughter about the mouth, at variance with the solemn, stately
> expression of the rest of his face.... He sat down and talked very
> naturally and freely, with a mixture of clear gushing accents in
> his voice, a deep gutteral intonation, and a strong tincture of the
> northern *burr,* like the crust on wine.

Hazlitt's Wordsworth of *Lyrical Ballads* is perhaps the most important witness poet of the post-French Revolutionary Period, writing beautifully about the poor and disenfranchised; he is the contemporary poet of ecology writing often about violence to nature, he is one of five major revisionists of Milton as epic poet, the other being Blake; indeed his visionary sense runs deep but is dialectically challenged by his commitment to religious institutions and land ownership.

I hope to refocus attention upon Wordsworth's acknowledgment in his poetic language of "the life of things," partly through running theme-and-variations on his poems and poetic language, partly through deformative strategies. My own ecological impulse is to recall to us the to me most generative elements in his poetry, as poets from Shelley to objectivists like Reznikoff and Niedecker to Ronald Johnson in *The Book of the Green Man* have already done.

READING AND TALKING with Barrett Watten and Carla Harryman
at the Naropa Summer Writing Program has been mind-blowing, and
by that term recalling the '60s I mean to suggest a convulsive turning
around, Achilles by the hair (!), about my intention for what I might call
this "Wordsworth project" (daybook and poetry as a way of proposing
currently unsaid things about this poet). Wordsworth (1815)/Fancy: *they*
want to keep Fancy out of serious poetics, and imagination does the "severe
keeping" out, which is a way of keeping out "impurities" of language: Thus
my "splices," etc. propose a return of impurities but in relation to modern
poetics, in an effort, I now see, to historicize, acknowledge, this time, my
time, as a cultural "moment" where new meanings are emerging. But I
can, I now see, do an analogous and perhaps historically more accurate
and shocking because less arbitrary thing by introducing "impurities" (e.g.
dialect) into Wordsworth from his own period (e.g. tail-rhyme poem for
WW, Burns, and Dorset!). *And* I want to revise my "May" poem to make
it even more radical by foregrounding even more the floating signifiers
like "blithe" and thinking further upon the manuscript variants which
include rather than, as the poems do, *exclude* movement and emergent
meaning. This then is taking the desynonymized Fancy of that poem and
making it self-conscious. Perhaps I could write a poem on "Lyre" that
reintroduces the "Emmeline" variant and makes the name, with its double
possibilities of referent (Dorothy and/or Emmeline Fisher) the contested
site of presence or absence. In my deformation of these poems I could
also emphasize the desynonymized I/me distinctions, the latter leading to
an emphasis upon the language itself. All of this reinforces my sense that
Wordsworth's late poetry of the Fancy contains within it the strong Fancy
of mobility and emergent meaning that his Orthodox Christianity and
perhaps his own paranoia about emergent meanings contradicted.

It is interesting that Leigh Hunt's desire to have Wordsworth bring
his world of country contemplation into the world of urban commodity

culture is his way of proposing a desynonomy of emergent meanings; it's also interesting to reflect (a la desynonomyzing/Zukofsky) on my very first entry of this journal about the juxtaposition of aristocratic form and "the poor." Hunt's poetry of the Fancy (and Keats's) is an attempt to make the Fancy a self-conscious presence; his translations call attention to language through translation as poetic deformation.

What is the meaning of Wordsworth's abandonment of the *LB* juxtaposition and poetic dialect for the *1807* poetry of animation beginning with the linguistic foundation flattenings in "Nutting" and "there was a boy"? In these 1800 pieces he collapses the "I" of identity into the language of identification. Perhaps I could do poems about this too. Notice that these poems occur in the volume where he drops anonymity and multiple authorships.

Think of Lucy poems, my readings of them, as the collapsing of "I" into "me" (the difference to me).

Is this the point of *1800*? Of *1800* as a deformation of *1798*?

And what of the *Poems on the Naming of Places* as an attempt to historicize poems in the landscape? To create moments of emergent meaning? And what of "spots of time" as moments in which "I" becomes "me"?

And later "Moods of my own mind" as also an effort to turn "I" into "me" (more poems on this), the emphasis on "similes" in the Daisy poem, in which the *vehicle* displaces the tenor put as "me" replaces "I." To focus so intensely upon a "mood" makes it an occasion of historical self-consciousness. One could look at W's 1800/1807 stanzas as juxtapositions analagous to the early ones rather than as closed containers. (Re-read reviews of *1807*.)

Our reading of Wordsworth must become much more self-conscious! Jerry McGann's argument that his poetry emphasized observation (i.e. focus on the referent) more than does STC's.

Consider (viz Watten's discussion of trauma and loss in Mayakofsky) the place of Wordsworth's early traumas and the poetry of "abundant recompense," with a real reading of "abundant" and "recompense" and both together.

Wordsworth's poetry of the "I" (the trauma) becomes a poetry of the "me," recompense for trauma that opens into emergent meaning of the "mood." It's not so much a retreat from the referent as the taking the fate of the poetic subject, a desynonymizing of it. Maybe he thought that STC couldn't travel with him here!

My notebook and project: a collage that attempts to turn the critical "I" into a critical/poetic "me."

Vernal Song of Blithe May

Between 1826 and 1835 William Wordsworth wrote two poems to the month of May. The following poem, however, builds on a careful review of the manuscripts of the May poems which show that the poet in his late 50s and early 60s had an intensely active and playful revisionary imagination. Here is a world that Wordsworth never wrote but that may have happened instantaneously and then faded into something more stable–we might call what follows a dream of the poems of May.

What cannot be conveyed here is how the two poems began as one short poem and then expanded to a very long poem before it settled into the final two. Also, the drafts show how vitally Wordsworth's images, lines, and stanzas *floated* and *flew* through different arrangements. Ought, for example, "blithe" go with "Flora" or with "May"? It leads one to reconsider him as a poet less of linear, irreversible directionality and more of a spatial imagination. Cf. Mandelstam: "poetry establishes itself with astonishing independence in a new extraspatial field of action." The cool elegance of Wordsworth's sentences and stanzas render the above-mentioned monochromaticity as banality. I have tried to catch the visionary possibilities of words like "hope," "blithe," "season," by placing them in a fast-moving stream or electric current.

Delicate veil renewed delicate veil
sweet May renewed delicate leafy veil
renewed in this deep dale delicate leafy
veil renewed sweet May blithe
May sweet May blithe May blithe
Flora blithe May blithe Flora blithe
May blithe blithe blithe Flora from
his couch upstarts blithe Flora blithe
May season blithe May season of
renewed delicate leafy blithe May
season of Fancy and Hope Season of
Fancy and of hope blithe May Season
of Fancy and fine touch of hope fine
touch of self-restraining self-restraining
art and hope Season of self-restraining
Season of Fancy and of hope tempering
tempering the years of extremes years extremes
tempering extremes extremes tempering
self-restraining breathes a freshness
A freshness breathes quickening quickening
where love nestles patient patient streams
inmost heart where love nestles
breathes freshness lustre and freshness
freshness lustre freshness lustre freshness
freshness o'er noonday lustre o'er noonday
stream that April could not check
could not check quickening lustre
scattering scattering scattering hope
scattering lustre blithe patient modest May
freshening glee scattering hope and lustre
scattering season of fancy entrust fancy

entrust unfinished song deathless song
deathless scattering song unfinished
breathes unfinished lustre of inmost heart
of quickening balance of delight How delicate
where love nestles how leafy blithe May
scattering lustres o'er noonday of unfinished
blessed sweet May sweet lustres blithe
May of deathless unfinished song

There was pleasure there.

Revised by Bob Perelman (or "literally translated," as he might say) to

Perhaps the desire to be wrong
Is the heart of wanting to write.
There must be some pleasure there.

WORDSWORTH'S SENTENCE IS A LITTLE HAMMOCK rocking back and forth between two trees, on each one he has attached the hammock with a "there." Perelman hates "elemental words," "last words," which hang the "late" Wordsworth in leaden orthodoxies. But hammocks are not elemental or last in Perelman's sense. The parentheses, the symmetry, refuse a *closure*, a la Gertrude Stein. This sentence refuses the unidirectional movement of the corporate sentence. One of the heroes of *The Prelude*, the "errant knight" saving stone and shell, conserves poetry and mathematics through his passionate wandering; perhaps the desire to be wrong/is the heart of wanting to write. "Be right" stands behind "write" as the rejected orthodoxy that poetry rejects. How subservient is Wordsworth to the lure of elemental language?

In his introduction to his selected poems, *Ten to One* (Middletown, Conn.: Wesleyan U. P., 1999), Perelman criticizes Wordsworth, particularly the "late," for his "lengthy claustrophobic halleluyahs" for the present movement. The usual critique: lofty, arrogant, complacent, monumental, and finally undemocratic—all because of an/or reflective of a pristine language that admits no impurity, no otherness, no argument. And no sex, no dream, no fakery and irreverence, no popular voice or gesture. He calls his introductory poem with its commentary "Fake Dream: the library, a very hip spot-of-time where the poet and his lover were heading for a clandestine fuck in the library ("sex in the stacks" voice alliterative binding of both the problem—keeping sex out of the canon—and the eventual solution—insisting upon it nevertheless in a kind of graffiti of the body). In a lovely Wordsworthian touch, he turns away ("Stop here, or gently pass!") temporarily from his intention to notice "the dark blue / spines of Wordsworth's *Collected*." Having meditated on the deficiencies of the canonical laureate of Rydal Mount, they wander into the men's room as a possible site for pleasure but are further arrested by the following graffiti:

> "This place needs
> a woman's touch" answered by "FINGER
>
> MY ASSHOLE, CUNT!" This second message
> had been modified by an arrow
>
> indicating "CUNT" was to be moved
> from behind to before "ASSHOLE": "FINGER
> MY CUNT, ASSHOLE!"

Leaving the men's room, they return to the stacks for sex, which occurs after the poem's close. The agon of graffiti becomes Perelman's emblem for effective poetry and in contrast to Wordsworth's: of the world, a mixture of voices, aggressively thoughtful and brilliant, itself composed of aggressively earthy slang, impure in the sense of highly inscripted, performative.

   Generally speaking, I take Perelman's point about elemental language and Wordsworth's affinity for it. But while the poem dramatizes the cutting-edge poetics of Language Poetry, it presents once again a tired view of Wordsworth—insight, yes, but much blindness too. About the earlier Wordsworth, he concedes: "Wordsworth was almost a democratic poet, almost an avant-gardist" (yes, and let's look more closely at the avant garde in Wordsworth), "But he achieved this at the cost of an idealized Nature, mute and female, and an infantilized sister...," clichés which are easy to refute. These observations have the effect of making "Wordsworth" a closed system admitting no possibility for observation and thought; they come from the fact that, in McGann's words, Wordsworth is perhaps the most "pre-read" of major poets, particularly the late (post-1820) Wordsworth where "pre-read" means "never read," but we all know about him and those sonnets "justifying capital punishment." Even if the cliché about Wordsworth is generally true, it doesn't help us engage all the references to a quickening power in this late poetry, or to a sense of mystery and spirituality in a language strangely susceptible to interesting deformations. Allen Grossman's statement that good poems contain aperture within closure I believe to be true for some of the late Wordsworth, a poetry we are finally in a position to acknowledge…and I suspect that Perelman knows some version of this, given the prominence given to Wordsworth in the Introduction to his poetic outpouring from 1975 to 1998 (curiously 200 years after *Lyrical Ballads*). This suggests an ambivalence about Wordsworth's poetry, which comes out similarly in his poem, "A Literal Translation of Virgil's Fourth Eclogue." There he is finally able to discover the prophetic poem of empire, a "lability," in the poem but very much in his own poetic response to it—as if "Empire" were a trauma to the imagination of a mind expecting to be free in the poem's presence. And in fact the shambles caused to imagination in the shape of "anxiety" produces, through the poet's patience and insistence, a new lability in which Virgil's *parve puer* becomes the poet's own child whose playfulness, much more than a "smile," is recounted in loving couplets. So Virgil moves forward, is drawn into the present, revisited and reanimated.

HAUNTING (VERB MORE THAN ADJECTIVE) bookstores. This lifetime
pleasure occasionally has yielded stunning, serendipitous results. The
subject of walking and its literature—walking a "haunting" as in Virginia
Woolf's "Street Haunting," with its sense of entering/creating states
of outsized, deformed conditions of perception—produced two such
biblioepiphanic moments. The first jump-started my walk-obsession:
walking into a bookstore near Salisbury Cathedral in 1972 (a store which
I revisited in 1998), I found a book I was apparently ready to find–to
stimulate a then new interest in walking literature. The nature of walking,
I'm sure, encouraged the sense of a chance encounter with *The Lore of the
Wanderer: An Open-Air Anthology*, edited by George Goodchild.

And the second occurred the day after I had read about Robert Walser,
who had written a not so short story called "The Walk." Haunting an
undistinguished, now long defunct used bookstore in South Denver, I found
a small volume, in a lightish blue dust-jacket, of Walser's *The Walk* trans.
Christopher Middleton. The book seemed to fly towards me; to purchase
it was pre-ordained, a celebration for mind and literary words, an embrace
that includes bookseller with author, me, and the poetic achievement
itself—a transcendental purchase.

Imagine opening a file drawer full of chapbooks and pamphlets at the
Hermitage Bookshop, Denver, directed by Joanne Weiss, who several years
ago planted them there, and seeing, in the W's, Keith &Rosemarie Waldrop

WORDS
WORTH
LESS.

Was it less than Wordsworth? Worth less than Wordsworth? Are words worth less than? Did these paragons of American/European avant gardism write something about/from Wordsworth? (This flurry and tumult happened yesterday 7/2/03.) Skimming through the chapbooks's eleven pages of letterpress text in italic fonts, I notice a scattering of familiar Wordsworthian words: e.g. form, memory, wanderings, for thy sake, green, steep, deeper, aching, dwelling, landscape, if, five years, flying, dream. And on the final page are the first four lines of "Tintern Abbey": "Five years have past...." The words cumulate, coalesce into six free-verse poems from "Tintern Abbey" very much like what I did in *The Life of Things: Utter Wordsworth*, except they returned to the poem five more times: theme and variations: symphony. Printed exactly 30 years ago (1973); of course I bought it, with that gratitude that shoots qualitatively past the ordinary experience of exchange.

As with my own, they make the poem "less," by emaciating the pentameter line, in both cases where the shortening of the line intends a trajectory towards the more precious which, as the line shrinks, anticipates zero and silence. Emphasizing "green" (e.g. "This green pastoral landscape"), both versions give the poem an ecological reading: Waldrops

> Motion and what's
> More,
> Form, that
> Is, the rather
> Green.

Our deformations drop Wordsworth's tricky domestic politics involving the mutual dependencies of the poet and the diarist Dorothy, sister and brother in prophetic mutual clinging. As the Waldrops' sequence develops, more of the phrases, as opposed to vocabulary, of "Tintern Abbey" take over, always skewed, to be sure, but insisting that the actual "Tintern Abbey" return to mind ("the picture of the mind revives again") in tension with the poem's new unfettered self.

If portion with that thought
These eyes, those gleams,
Then on the banks together I so long a
Rather say, far deeper.

They leave out "worshiper of nature" ("I so long a worshiper of nature"), so the "I" swims in the shallow stream of various words. In both versions the "I" loses its solid pentameter table, that "less"ening more evident in my poem:

a green
spirit
rolls
through all
blue
things

a coarser
pleasure
rolls through
setting
suns

vagrant
murmurs
no trivial
impressed
silence
one
rolling

language of

sneers

nursed in

prayer

bless the

fever

suspended

faint hung

dim shapes

of cities

green gleam

what was

        green I

        fretful

        have I

        felt gifts:

        mournful

bounding

        dizzy

        gone

        gifts?

STUDENTS IN MY NAROPA COURSE on deforming poems wrote deformations of "The Solitary Reaper." Here is one by Stefani Iryne:

> *rearrange in thirds*
> old things
>   perhaps numbers
> the more familiar
>
>   if endings
>   could be motion-
>   less
> breaking   a single field
> melancholy is bending
>
>   what   one
> heard
>   after
>   singing
>   binds her
>   maiden

Stephani's new poem is Wordsworth without a first-person subject and without a narrative of self. The archaic ("old things") frames and haunts the breaking up of voice. Indeed "breaking" stands at the poem's center, no longer bird-song breaking the silence of the seas, but now far more ambiguous ("melancholy"? "a single field"?) and elemental—a breaking that releases, or frees, silence and space on the page. The visual opening of the poem meshes with, even more than in the original, a meditative voice— this poem now is truly an *imago vocis*—an image, not a lyric narrative or drama. The last isolated, constelled words shape an after-singing, perhaps

139

unheard melodies, but surely a Wordsworthian legacy of poetic effect, a vision of reverberations from poetic activity. Yes, very Wordsworthian, an "alien sound of melancholy."

This after-singing, moreover, settles finally not on some male speaker rapidly vanishing like Rilke's Orpheus into the upper air, but on the poem's female presence, a maiden.

In a beautiful passage from her deformation of the same poem, Leigh Thornhill transforms the conventional sadness of endings: here "endings" at least in poetry are a construction:

> i hear
>
> the sound of
>
> endings over
>
> flowing in
>
> your voice

This allows for an uncanny rewriting of the speaker's permanent distance from the reaper, which the poem seems to build in, to a song of direct address announcing permanent connection through song.

> First there is a pain—of love and desire?—
>> you cut gently
>
>> my heart
>
>> still
> but ends
>> you will sing
>> i will sing
>> of far off things
>
> a single profound sound
>> binding no more
>> time after today.

"There is a spot"

Who, in Wordsworth, declares, "There is"? A voice observes, knows, transmits or trans-lates a scene—with what authority? From what position? All we can say is that his is a voice of fancy-apprehension. He knows "seems," he knows figures like the simile and other comparisons and his mind ranges wide; he's willing to entertain contradictions. Consider "The Danish Boy" composed in 1799, published in the expanded 1800 *Lyrical Ballads*, in which this disembodied voice (cf. Geoffrey Hartman) finds a "spot" of mysterious song, a tropism for what swells in its unknowability. The voice declares and describes and doesn't disturb. Why, one wonders, does he think anyone would be interested? Perhaps a reader would discover him-/herself in a spot that included this voice and attentiveness to something, presented in simple tetrameter, familiar/unfamiliar, approachable/unapproachable, of the world/only of the poem's words.

> Between two sister moorland hills
> There is a spot that seems to lie
> Sacred to the flowrets of the hills,
> And sacred to the sky.

I can't help it: this is a perfect piece (intentionless?) of poetry, a perfect frame to initiate the five 11-line stanzas that construct an outrageously liminal domain. The speaker directs us to a cleft in the visible, or, less an absence and more the substance of a betweenness. The finality of the copulative ("there is") is flavored with the engagement of witness ("seems"), an insistence upon the warmth of the crisis of human perception. But with the vividness of voice of personality and precision of place comes a (contrary?) attentiveness to the poetry of the thing:

> ...seems to lie
> sacred....

Before it crosses the enjambed line break, the words might indicate a) the imperfectness of perception and b) the possibility of deception. So within the flat certainty of "there is" lies a turbulence of uncertainty and even mendacity that the space at line end reinforces. But then the verse turns back to the next line opening with the stressed "sacred," a word that by its nature flies beyond the spiritual control of who utters it. From "sacred" *flows* the next two lines which direct us away from, past, with no reference to, "the human":

> Sacred to flowrets of the hills,
> And sacred to the sky.

Flowerets and sky become registers of value, of the spiritual, which find their locus in this "spot," so precisely general but apparently beaming its sacredness outward. The voice in this poem exhibits no paranoia in the completely self-sufficient other-directedness of what it perceives. The clean, boxy tetrameter stands "between" the speaker and what he/she engages with.

Poetically, the formal elements create an "impermeability" (Bernstein), another take on liminality, that allows a loosening of a potential affective grip that the weirdness of the scene might produce, a kind of vertiginous fall through the lines (as often happens in 18th-century Pindaric and forms of sentimental verse) into the event.

For a "ballad," even a lyrical ballad, this one eschews narrative at every turn. The Danish boy has a history and sings of other histories in a "forgotten tongue," but the poem, with great discipline, keeps them out of sight and sound, in order to observe. On the boundary of narrative, the poem is indifferent to that for which generally it has such a historically primary affinity. Here are the first two and the last stanzas:

> Between two sister moorland rills
> There is a spot that seems to lie
> Sacred to flowrets of the hills,
> And sacred to the sky.
> And in this smooth and open dell

There is a tempest-stricken tree;
A corner-stone by lightning cut,
The last stone of a cottage hut;
And in this dell you see
A thing no storm can e'er destroy,
The shadow of a Danish Boy.

In clouds above, the lark is heard,
He sings his blithest and his best;
But in this lonesome nook the bird
Did never build his nest.
No beast, no bird hath here his home;
The bees borne on the breezy air
Pass high above those fragrant bells
To other flowers, to other dells,
Nor ever linger there.
The Danish Boy walks here alone:
The lovely dell is all his own....

There sits he:–in his face you spy
No trace of a ferocious air,
Nor ever was a cloudless sky
So steady or so fair.
The lovely Danish Boy is blest
And happy in his flowery cove;
From bloody deeds his thoughts are far;
And yet he warbles songs of war;
They seem like songs of love,
For calm and gentle is his mien;
–Like a dead Boy he is serene.

Exhausting to write about this poem! And haven't even gotten to the Danish Boy himself. But the discussion of him is descriptive to the point that you realize the liminality of the description of a person: a potential or expected ballad of linear narrative is instead a cumulating constellation of attributes: one witnesses what one sees and knows, without plunging into the story of the other. A change from the witness poems of Blake, Robinson, Southey, and Wordsworth himself in the 1790s. Instead witness and object blend into a *language between them*:

> And in this dell you see
> A thing no storm can e'er destroy,
> The shadow of a Danish Boy.

The poem never breaks into Danish, into archaism, dialect, no virus or impurity of speech: a deficiency many would say. But the language is always already a "forgotten tongue," a wonderfully metaphoric rendering of the absent body of the absent speech, the substantiality of an oblivion. (Cf. Rilke's Eurydice, Sie war schon Wurzel.) At the same time ("And yet"), "there is" a knowledge of this forgottenness:

> From bloody deeds his thoughts are far;
> And yet he warbles songs of war,
> That seem like songs of love,...

The calm acknowledges a trauma, collective or personal somewhere in a past, but "Fancy" has converted it into its opposite, love. Could the poem itself be a "song of love," a full map of acknowledgment, an engagement with an unknowing? Where what one sees and thinks overwhelms an unknown history? And how fine a poetic enterprise; the acknowledgment of the absolute, traumatic Real by constructing a betweenness of shadows of beauty and pleasure: the haunted pleasure of saying "there is."

In his 1807 *Poems, in Two Volumes*, Wordsworth wrote a footnote to one of three poems called "To a Daisy": "the two following poems were overflowings of the mind in composing the one that stands first in the first Volume." (*P, 2V* p.238) OVERFLOWINGS OF THE MIND! Except for the phrase "spontaneous overflow of powerful feelings," and even in that phrase, we do not think of Wordsworth as a poet of overflowings, of excess. But here it is: the note, in fact, describes a process not untypical of his late poetic practice, where one could list quite a few important poems cut out of an overflow of poetry: one long poem becomes two or more shorter ones. In this "Daisy" poem ("With little here to do or see…") overflow has a formal expression as a parataxis of similes about the daisy (a practice that anticipates a similar simile overflow in Shelley's visionary poem "to a Skylark"):

> Oft do I sit by thee at ease,
> And weave a web of similes,
> Loose types of things through all degrees,
>   Thoughts of thy raising:
> And many a fond and idle name
> I give to thee, for praise or blame,
> As is the humour of the game,
>   While I am gazing.

Note the rhyme:

                at ease
        web of similes
Things through all degrees.

1807 connects ease and leisure with not a trope but the proliferation of tropes, things, and thoughts. Another section of *1807* is called "Moods of My Own Mind," as if "mood" itself becomes a sub-genre of poem analogous to "apostrophe" or "prayer" or "invocation." A poetry of the person-at-ease sunken in a worldly stillness, a reclining posture of inactivity that also is a performance (look, I sit at ease!) where "I is the other," one sitting at ease thwarting identity-in-labor under the control of the market economy but erupting with energy from and also to another domain. The reviewers of *1807* asked defensively: why should we be interested in Mr. Wordsworth's moods? And one answer is: they are not precisely *his* moods: these are not poems of "identity" but of "identification," an *imago* of the voice of the mood, or a performance of a mood, one which emits a great deal of imaginative energy and thus enters the long tradition of a poetry of *otium* that endangers a society of Protestant work ethic and, in a more contemporary vein, follows in the spirit of French Revolutionary thought: any one can be free to think and expand at one's ease.

Burns's "To a Mountain Daisy" stands one generation behind Wordsworth's daisy poem, and I find it far more compelling than any of Wordsworth's daisy pieces. The idyllic moments in Wordsworth's versions mask the harsh vulnerability of Burns's, formally the clipped, intensely rhythmic tail-rhyme stanzas of Burns get puffed into the later poet's eight-line stanza of leisured play. The tragic urgency of "To a Mountain Daisy" becomes a social urgency, a passion about poetry and democracy, about the ethical need to notice and support the unnoticed in society as well as in nature. To show ecological sensitivity is to acknowledge as well the socially disenfranchised. But I need to caution myself against simply contrasting Wordsworth's daisy as an occasion for his complacency because his daisy poems image a person with imagination playful and alive in the presence of a flower, a mind and senses expansive and experimentally dwelling both on a flower and on a mood.

Having said that, I find Burns imaginatively dazzling in its visionary leap in the domain of scarcity: both poems are apostrophes, but Burns addresses the cut, or dead flower rather than living daisies; it's harder to feel the pathetic fallacy argument (were one so inclined) with Burns's more complex poetic situation of a consciousness that he has destroyed the thing he wants to praise (conserve). The Scots dialect in the stanzas trained on the flower emphasize the flower's otherness and distinctness, like a member of an ethnic minority, a woman, a poet: the speaker praises the daisy in the language of the other rather than the "purer" standard English used when he translates the flower's tragedy into that of other members of society.

Ever since I wrote about "To a Mountain Daisy" in *Romantic Presences* (1995), I've been taken with the focus on the daisy's *stem*:

> Wee, modest, crimson-tipped flow'r,
> Thou's met me in an evil hour;
> For I maun crush among the stoure
> > Thy tender stem:
> To spare thee now is past my pow'r,
> > Thou bonie gem.
>
> Alas, it's no thy neebor sweet,
> > The bonie *Lark*, companion meet!
> > > Wi' spreckl'd breast,
> When upward-springing, blythe, to greet
> > > The purpling East.

As I wrote once before:

> The crisis of the daisy resides in its superb stem–rising out of the earth or raising the flower itself up, bending under the singing weight of the lark, and crushed by the plow. Let us call a poem a bending stem; conforming to another pressure which (the lark) has song and an infinity of metaphor in it, and yet creating with the pressure its own peculiar arc–the image of a tension and release of sound, at once the wavering and secure beauty of rootedness and a not-self, the singing flying color of the bird, a tropism not the daisy but the upspringing lark. Energies originate in the flower the earth the bird the sun and the adversary cold and dry-and-rockiness and wind. The poem: an event or object of multiple energy centers, yet revealing in its materiality itself as a bending stem singing.

Butterfly

                         self-pois'd

                           upon a daisy

self-pois'd   gone   return

                         stem motion

I once   Unblest hover

     about their diaphanous crust

Heron

                       itself

                       from

     Rydal Water:

                       paper slapping

days before London

                       arcing

     beautiful

                       bird-song

                        I cry out

   clawing

                       a daisy

Having observed that Wordsworth's daisy poems vanquish the social significance made so poignant and urgent by Burns (a standard critique of Wordsworth), one needs to assert–as I have tried to do in these poems–the independent life in the Grasmere poet's encounter with daisies.

"The Unremitting Voice of Nightly Streams"

DID WORDSWORTH GROW OLD, poetically that is, as the tradition has claimed he did: famous, pompous, and writing sonnets advocating capital punishment? Enough said?—

Yes, but "this will never do" for the old version of "my William Wordsworth." The poet of such emphatic closures and "elemental" (in Watten's bad sense of language shorn of its social and ethnic, its local, features) language still contains aperture within it. The life of things in late Wordsworth (say, crudely, from 58 until death at 80) lives, is transmitted into new form, discourse, and images, into new vision, and into, from time to time, an intensely playful practice of writing and revision. (If he could have composed on computer, much of interest would have vanished.) The early practice of composing while walking/muttering *The Prelude* (1802-1805) continues at Rydal Mount with the path made between the great house and summer hut. Muttering, a near stream of words, seems to have followed him as a career-long practice. (He even muttered his way to "Tintern Abbey.") This streamy speech—the length of a footpath or a Blake fourteener or a long-line of Whitman—ur-language of poetry that surrounds the globe, today vying we know not how successfully, with the e-wave pollution, and has since Orpheus and Philomela. Rumi, they say, delivered poetry in a stream; only his recording angels made the social, inscribed line so that readers could read.

Poetry as inscription: the lovers' wound on and of the bark of the tree (Marvell), the translation of the ur-poetry (Wordsworth's leech gatherer, a stream scarce heard) into the world of history and sociality. A way of locating late Wordsworth on this map! he went too far into the inscribed: his poetry is too much in history and not enough in its far precincts, where words trail off into music ("upper limit") and life-giving water. Yet two or three massive moments, or *nodes* seem to structure the years of 1828 to

1834 and again 1841–1842, vortices of poetic turbulence, process and/as fruition. To get to the wildness, however, you need the manuscripts where the watery—that is, streamy, oceanic, or lake-like—aspects take over. Poems (cf. the May poems *supra*) divide and join or rejoin, words float from home to home blank verse and heroic couplets stream then island themselves. Titles appear only to vanish. Originals in Wordsworth's (the term is painfully apt) crabbed hand give way to then clean elegance of a Sara Hutchinson fair copy that in turn receives the poet's thick black cross-outs and more crabbed revisions. Revisions appear over or under the original or they can run up the left hand margin. In at least one instance (Dove Cottage Manuscript 89, 91v and 92r), "The Unremitting Voice of Nightly Streams," the collision of several poems produces something visual, spatial—a conjunction of streams, a collage of poems: along with the above are bits of "On the Power of Sound," "The Somnambulist," and "The Triad." "On the Power of Sound" begins with its twelfth (out of thirteen) sections. Different hands are at work, a community of pens, crossouts, asterisks, writing up the margin. All the fever looks like a form of action painting.

And yet the poetry is about THE ONE, THE HOLY:

> There is a world of Spirit
> The unremitting *voice* (emphasis mine) of nightly streams.

If the holy appears as singular, the poetic appears as multiple, a tension utterly vital in this MS.

Not one but many voices (revisions, poems) stream together here, never adding up to *one*.

Let me work my way to the poem.

An early version of opening line:

> The unsuspended voice of mountain streams

Which eventually settled into

> The unremitting voice of nightly streams.

Both exhibit the trademark Wordsworthian double negative: not suspended or hung up, not remitted or sent back. Mountain, simple place descriptor; nightly, locates the voice in time, but in a strangely adverbial way: sounding at night? A stream with the quality of nightliness? Have you heard a nightly stream? If there is any sound of poetry's primal, ur-language, it is here. Listening, I am absorbed in its stillness-in-motion, Dauer im Wechsel; it alludes to the day gone by, just as "remit" alludes to the world of financial exchange and also of disease (a suspension of cancer's aggressivity), a haunting of the sound of stillness.

The rest of the poem, in all versions, declares that this voice, while not affecting the animal and vegetable kingdoms, can "regulate" the human heart, mind, and soul in sleep (like the "spots of time" with their silent, renovating virtue). At one stage of the poem, it introduces another narrative called "The Somnambulist," that features a knight who, imaging he has caused the madness and death of his beloved, "built a cell" and "In hermits' weeds repose he found…Beside the torrent dwelling bound/By one deep heart-controlling sound." It's that voice that gives the distracted hermit solace through "regulation" of his dreams. In the final version that knight has vanished in order to turn the poem into a general statement about this "power of sound" throughout time and throughout social classes.

In 1826–1828 Wordsworth had befriended the popular poet Felicia Hemans, who wrote a beautiful poem "To Wordsworth," praising precisely his capacity to recover in verse the "sources of life."

> Thine is a strain to read among the hills,
>   The old and full of voices,–by the source
> Of some free stream, whose gladdening presence fills
>   The solitude with sound; for in its course
>
>
> Even such is thy deep song, that seems a part
> Of those high scenes, a fountain from their heart....
> True bard and holy!–thou art e'en as one
>   Who, by some secret gift of soul or eye,
> In every spot beneath the smiling sun,
>   Sees where the springs of living waters lie:
> Unseen awhile they sleep–till, touched by thee,
> Bright healthful waves flow forth, to each glad wanderer free.

They must have conversed upon the question of poetry as waste, and the beauty of pleasures afforded by nature as waste. A meaningful, perhaps intimate poetic subject for the 57-year-old Wordsworth, a monument whose monumental poems might at times have seemed a distraction, brought on, to be sure, by himself, from the unmoored, or winged, reverie-drenched discourse of the life of things. Waste: a tantalizing topic for poetry; for Georges Bataille, waste and excess define the sacred in poetry, that which can't be *put to use*. Hemans, no longer primarily a writer of massive historical poems and plays, had turned to delicate lyrics of expiration: we value the expiring breath (the "last song") precisely because it thins and dissipates. In "Night-Blowing Flowers" (1827) a wanderer petitions these flowers to save their lovely odours for the life of the day instead of wasting them in the presence of all sleeping things. The flowers answer:

Call it not wasted, the scent we lend

   To the breeze when no step is nigh;

Oh! thus for ever the earth should send

   Her grateful breath on high!

Shift the coordinates of value from the human / natural to the human / divine and the "faint perfume" of night-blowing flowers signifies on "the silent shine of night."

Wordsworth, I imagine, would have joined eagerly (initiated? followed?) discussion of the holy in poetry: how to justify (guilt!) then treasure poetry as waste. The several versions of the second line of "The unremitting voice" reveal the struggle to define, to acknowledge (as a prophet) the power of the sound of nightly streams.

1) The unremitting voice of mountain streams

   That calls the breeze to modulate its powers

2) The unsuspended voice of mountain streams

   Where Nature seems to work with wasted powers

3) The unsuspended voice of mountain streams

   Tires not the day nor wastes on night its powers

4) The unremitting

   The unsuspended\ing Voice of mountain streams

   Where Nature works, we think, with wasted powers

5) The unremitting voice of nightly mountain streams

   That wastes so oft, we think, its tuneful / soothing powers

The poem tries to lift itself out of the human perspective ("seems" "we think") to map out the divine, which is simultaneously the unconscious trajectory that provides a cosmic coherence (modulate, regulate) of blessed control, but that also comes from a vitality acting with or without our awareness. Reading the final published version, a pentameter 17-line poem with one short line, one is tempted to attribute to the poet an aesthetic modesty yielding before the grandeur of a divine pathway between nature and human subjects, a regulation surpassing the aesthetic. The poem, however, is one highly tortured sentence that loses itself in appositive, parenthetical, and inverted structures, hardly the "elemental" syntax befitting a poet laureate.

> The unremitting voice of nightly streams
> That wastes so oft, we think, its tuneful powers,
> If neither soothing to the worm that gleams
> Through dewy grass, nor small birds hushed in bowers,
> Nor unto silent leaves and drowsy flowers,—
> That voice of unrelenting harmony
> (For who what is shall measure by what seems
> To be, or not to be,
> Or tax high Heaven with prodigality?)
> Wants not a healing influence that can creep
> Into the human breast, and mix with sleep
> To regulate the motion of our dreams
> For kindly issues–as through every clime
> Was felt near murmuring brooks in earliest time;
> As at this day, the rudest swains who dwell
> Where torrents roar, or hear the tinkling knell
> Of water-breaks, with grateful heart could tell.

But place this poem in relation to the double-manuscript pages of DCMS 89, consider the poem not unsuspended for 18 years, consider the confluence of two famous poets on the subject of poetry and waste and confluence of poems:

> "The Triad," light-hearted playful occasion piece to daughter
> and her friends

"On the Power of Sound," abstract and philosophical and
theological, the sequel in his mind to the "Immortality Ode"
"The Somnambulist," tale of the tragedy of passion

and

"The Unremitting Voice," itself, a visionary account, from a
disembodied voice, of emanations of driving beneficence in nature.
A collage, a quilt of poetic possibilities, energy flaring on the page.

> At the bottom of the lake is a small stream
> of black liquid. A sentence assumes more
> than it admits.

(Barrett Watten, from *Decay*, 1977)

wasted Voice calls the breeze
nightly so oft nightly
   we think

            we think

                     we

                              think

            we think
wasted
         the unremitting voice seems
                     and tires not
mountain wastes unremitting powers
spend nightly
            emitting streams
soothing and
tuneful   suspended waste

155

unremitting streams spend

    soothing to modulate

                      waste

    tuneful waste

Nature calls wasted powers tuneful of waste

we suspend nightly waste of unVoice

That calls the breeze where Nature nightly works

Day tires not nor suspends

The unremitting voice of nightly streams

    with tuneful

             wasted

                   powers.

(to be or or or not to be or or or to be

(not to be to be or not to be to be or not to be

IN MY DEFORMATION of "'The Unremitting Voice of Nightly Streams'"
I hope to reveal (critical, secondary poetry reveals as it deforms) not only
waste as excess but also a remarkable obsession with "negativity," in the
Lacanian and Zizekian sense of an absolute "Real" of a traumatic source. In
light of the obsessively "positive" nature of Wordsworth's late poetry that
emits nothing but the Official Story of Anglican Christianity, this poem's
relentless allusion to the negative (particularly when one acknowledges
a manuscript, pre-publication life of at least eighteen years) becomes an
extraordinary account of concern for poetry's calling to image as negatives
and epistemologically pessimistic formulations the triumph of a *non-positive*
displacement of traumatic origin(s). Here human life is envisioned as
potentially survivable and coherent, potentially loving, in the face of, out
of, a huge destructive turbulence. In Wordsworth's case this might include
the death-days of parents and the "holocaust" of the September Massacres
of 1792 (cf. *The Prelude*, X) with the paranoid sense of probable return of
that holocaust. But this important late poem refuses to locate the Real
in these particular historical events (perhaps in DCMS 89, 91r, 92v, this
refusal is embodied in the decision, over time, to eliminate from the poem
the allusion to the beloved's drowning herself and the consequent self-
isolation of her lover). Wordsworth has often been faulted for a refusal to
grant more concreteness and visibility to the Other, but in the terms I am
considering, this refusal allows a greater freedom of mind—the presence of
the utterly compelling and absorbing Other (cf. Dante the pilgrim's limited
access to knowledge of the Other in the Inferno). This freedom, accorded
to Wordsworth and generally to experimental poetry, is the central privilege
and requirement of poetry's relationship to the object.

   This poem, when looked at even in its final, published version but
more drastically with the chaos of manuscripts written over nearly two
decades, enacts both the juxtaposition of parts of different poems and in
the torturous sentence that is the final poem the turbulence and near loss

of control that writing about the absolute negative Real seems to require. To me this poem, in its entire history, is itself a kind of "Wordsworth notebook," a manifestation of his genuineness as a poet.

Wordsworth as guide: "listen to the language in nightly streams; the ur-language that heals by linking us to the sources of life—'to soothe' or heal does not exclude 'to stimulate' the mind, but that connection requires the labor of consciousness against the tendency—brought about by the market ('use') and institutional religion (the safe and familiar) and war and oppression (a drowsy numbness)–towards oblivion, towards forgetfulness. I am susceptible to all of these complacencies, yet I know the holiness of poetry as waste and play, even in painful confusion, as a healing pleasure of mind."

Poem on the letter "A"

(from "The Triad," 1828)

        Triad

Naiad   Dryad

        Dora

Sara   Lucida

       MAY

fancy

  pathless

  command

    (hand in hand)

       coral Ida

interweavings waving:

  earth and sea

  measure aery

  starry

   Lady

        near

  fair tear

       day

  archer

   heavenly day

  hath   Majesty

A canopy

vainly

lagging

shades sang

           raftered

  delicate

        dance

       ungarlanded

       breathed

Idolian

  Thracian

        arch audacity

         primal

aim

       star vague

       Daughter

as faery clapping

Last

       skylark's

        gladness a float.

Dawn fair page a hand

  azure

  angels

  all fragrance

THERE WAS PLEASURE THERE

Printed in the United States
34113LVS00005B/1-75

9 781581 771022